Graham Tuckley is a retired senior lecturer in Social Work. His formative working years were spent in the Royal Navy and his memoirs of this time are set out in this book. After leaving the Royal Navy, he worked with disadvantaged children, working in residential settings before qualifying as a social worker. After 30 years working in the field of social work and gaining numerous academic qualifications, including an MSc in Health and Social Care, he turned his interest to teaching. He still resides in Walsall, spending time writing, gardening, and travelling.

This book has been inspired by my nephews and nieces who never stop to amaze me with continuous achievements and their maturity. I dedicate this book to them, my brothers and sisters-in law, extended family, friends and to all those people who served with me during the 1970s and to all those still serving or who have served in the Royal Navy. I hope that what I have produced will be of interest to many of you.

Graham Stuart Tuckley

SHIPS, TRIPS AND RITES OF PASSAGE

A SAILOR'S TALE

AUSTIN MACAULEY PUBLISHERS™

LONDON • CAMBRIDGE • NEW YORK • SHARJAH

A CIP catalogue record for this title is available from the British Library.

ISBN 9781398458918 (Paperback)
ISBN 9781398463318 (Hardback)
ISBN 9781398464599 (ePub e-book)

www.austinmacauley.com

First Published 2022
Austin Macauley Publishers Ltd®
1 Canada Square
Canary Wharf
London
E14 5AA

I would like to acknowledge and thank my nephew Paul and niece Joanne, who first read my initial manuscript and who encouraged me to publish this work. I would also like to thank Austin Macauley Publishers for their commitment to this work and for their support throughout.

Table of Contents

Chapter One
New Entry

Monday, 4 May 1970, saw the day I left my home in the Midlands for what would be a short but productive service in Her Majesty's Royal Navy. I had only just reached my sixteenth birthday and I was off on an adventure of a lifetime. It had only been three weeks since my sixteenth birthday but this was to be the start of the building of my character and of the person who I am today. Little did I know just how profound an effect this time and experience was to have on me and how much this time would impact the rest of my life. The discipline I was to receive as a result of joining Her Majesty's Forces enabled me to achieve much, even long after I had left the Navy, in terms of how I present myself to the world and how I was able to succeed professionally. My days in the navy have always remained fixed firmly in my heart and thoughts over the years and each day through my life, something from those days has popped up daily to guide my way.

I left home having said goodbye to my four brothers, their wives and children and made my way to the railway station. I was accompanied to Birmingham New Street train station by my mother and my then girlfriend Gail. My mother had signed for me to join the navy, at my behest, after I had visited a forces' exhibition at Bingley Hall in Birmingham. On the way home from the exhibition, I called into the Navy Recruitment Office that was then situated in New Street Station. The recruitment officer was so enthusiastic about the navy that some of his enthusiasm rubbed off on me and I returned home begging my mother to let me join.

After some discussion, my mother said, "If this is what you really want to do, then I will not stop you, but remember, it will not be easy."

The papers from the Royal Navy recruitment office arrived and my mother signed as I had requested. Within days, my orders came through to begin my training at HMS Raleigh in Devon.

On the day of my departure, my mother, girlfriend and I travelled first by bus, then local train to Birmingham New Street where I exchanged my travel warrant, provided by the navy for my train journey. I also collected platform tickets for my mother and girlfriend Gail. I had known Gail since school and we were more best friends than boyfriend/girlfriend, although everyone saw us as a couple. On the platform, little was said whilst we waited for the train to take me away from home and family. So quiet were we that it appeared we were lost in our own thoughts. Apart from the obligatory;

"You promise that you'll write?"

"Yes, I promise."

"You've got everything?"

"Yes, I have."

"Are you sure this is what you want?"

"Yes it is." None of us really conversed.

The train arrived on time steaming along the platform and stopping precisely so that passengers could disembark and alight. I boarded the train, called the Cornishman and made my way along the train to my carriage. At approximately 09:30, the train began to move. I was hanging out of the window waving vigorously and shouting bye to my mother and to Gail, who were reciprocating but who were both in floods of tears. The train surged forward with whistle blowing and great billows of steam gushed from below the main engine. Soon the train was gone from the station and I could not see my mother or Gail.

The Cornishman had departed from Bradford at 07:06, going first to Leeds, then calling at Manchester, Crew and on to Birmingham. The train was due to arrive at Plymouth at 15:08, stopping on the way at Bristol Temple Meads and Exeter before ending its journey at Plymouth where I would be getting off.

Although the farewell at the station was very moving and tearful, and the waving of goodbyes endless until the train was out of sight, it was also a very exciting day for me. On boarding the train and within minutes I met up with other 16- and 17-year-old young men, all travelling to Plymouth and all joining the Navy on the same day. It was interesting to note just how quickly we gelled. Our mood was high and the conversation was centred on what we thought it would be like to be in HM Forces and what we had all being doing prior to joining.

There were lots of laughs along the way too with many of the guys cracking jokes and providing stories of past girlfriends and of minor involvements with the law. I was immediately attracted to one young man from Stoke-on Trent, who stood out from the crowd. This young man had a front tooth missing as did I, but was able to project a beaming smile that was infectious. Pugh was to become a trusted friend throughout our initial training as raw recruits and remained my friend until we parted company on joining our first ships. Pugh was also very handsome in a boyish kind of way and appeared very fit. Apparently Pugh was good at rugby and enjoyed anything sporty.

At 15:08 precisely, the Cornishman slowly pulled into Plymouth station. We disembarked, and were immediately met by Petty Officer Lewis. POME Lewis (Petty Officer Marine Engineering Lewis) was a dark haired Welshman. Pugh and I were placed in separate groups because each group was organised by name alphabetically. Groups of 15 were led to awaiting trucks. I was quite taken aback when I saw that each of the transporters were all painted Navy Blue and had their own specialised number plates, for example; 12RN34. By 15:45, the trucks were filled to capacity and they moved in convoy through the City of Plymouth. On-board were new recruits from Scotland, Northumberland, Yorkshire, Lancashire, Cheshire, Cumbria, Wales, London, the Midlands, the West Country and other places across the United Kingdom. After what seemed to be an hour or more of travelling, yet still excited, we pulled into a large parking area in Devonport to catch the Torpoint Ferry. Here we were told to get off the trucks and make our way to the ferry on foot. For many, this was to be their very first experience of being on water. Although the ferry crossing only took a few minutes, about ten in total, one of our new shipmates became violently sick. I am not sure whether he suffered from sea sickness or whether this was a delayed reaction from travelling in one of the RN transport trucks. At the point of disembarking from the ferry, we were ushered back onto the Royal Navy transport trucks and were taken the one and a half miles to our final location HMS Raleigh.

HMS Raleigh, was commanded by Captain James FR Weir RN, and was the new entry and engineering training establishment for all new entry ratings to the Royal Navy and where raw recruits were first processed. Younger rating entrants or boy recruits were sent to HMS Ganges. From the early 1950s, HMS Raleigh had been the training base for ratings at new entry and for engineering for stoker mechanics.

At the entrance gate of HMS Raleigh, all new ratings were 'checked in', as no one was allowed past the base gates without an ID badge or letter of confirmation. Our first port of call was the New Entry Galley, where food and hot drinks were provided in abundance. Feeding approximately 120 new recruits was the Navy's first priority it seemed.

One guy said, "Don't drink the tea."

He had been informed by his father (who had completed National Service) that Bromide is added to the tea to prevent raw recruits from getting an erection and to stop any unnecessary sexual activity. I remember thinking that I must be safe, as I had always disliked tea and only drank coffee and further thinking that any form of sexual activity was a definite 'no no', particularly when in training and in barracks.

After being fed, we were marched to the New Entry Division. We all carried our civilian bags which had been limited by contents following written instruction prior to leaving home and taken into a large room within the New Entry Block. Here, we were given the number of the sleeping hall that we were to be located and instructions of what the next day would bring. We were then led off to our respective sleeping halls and told to find a bed. There were 15 beds to each hall, all having bedding folded neatly at the foot of each bed. To the right of the bed was a small silver coloured locker. We were told to place our bags in our locker and were then instructed on how to make our bed. Making beds is not the easiest thing for some. We had to ensure that the bottom sheet was straight and looking as if it had just been ironed, this turned out to be tricky for some. Then the making of hospital corners threw some guys completely off guard. Blankets were placed, followed by the counterpane, a decorative top cover made of cotton that resembled the willow pattern on dinner plates but which had anchors and ropes as decoration.

We were then instructed to get our towels, undress and go for a shower. Embarrassment filled the room as each new recruit stripped and placed their towels around their waist. We were all told to fold our civilian clothes neatly and place these on top of our lockers. We were instructed to get pyjamas ready and to ensure that we all had clean pants, socks and shirt ready for the following morning. We were led to the showers where a Leading Hand ('killick', a rating equivalent to corporal in the Army) was waiting to show us all how to wash properly. Washing included how your hair should be washed, how to wash your hands and to remove dirt from under the finger nails, washing of the body and genitals, legs and by far the most important, your feet. The washing and care of feet was a real issue for raw recruits, as for the majority of the time, we would be marching, running and doing lots and lots of physical activities where feet would get very wet, very sore and which helped in reducing foot-related medical problems.

After showering, we were taken back to our sleeping hall, told to prepare for bed and informed that we would be called at 5:30 am for roll call. The motto 'early to bed, early to rise' sprang to mind. Once all in our respective beds, we were bade 'goodnight' and the lights were switched off. Much giggling and silly noises were made for the first hour or so, but eventually all was quiet and people slept.

At 5:30 am on the dot, lights were switched on, a booming voice shouted; "Hands off cocks and on with socks."

"Get up you lazy bastards, it's nearly the middle of the day."

With some moans and gowns, the new recruits began to slowly sit up and get out of bed.

"Right you lot, time for a shower, then get dressed and be ready for breakfast by 6:15 am."

As ordered, our group began toileting, showering and dressing. We only just made the 6:15 deadline and many were still half asleep, including me. After being taken to the Galley, we were provided with breakfast, most avoided the tea, but the food was good and substantial. We were taken back to the New Entry meeting hall. Here we were given instruction again about what would be happening during our first days in New Entry. The first week would be taken up with physical checks; medical and dental, hair cutting, kit maintenance and marking, general Navy Values, drill and basic seamanship training not including any technical work.

We were supplied with a book of rules and regulations and a seaman's manual. We were told to read and digest what was in these texts and informed that we would be tested on our knowledge at the end of the week. We were given a guided tour of HMS Raleigh with directions that had to be memorised. We were told where we could and could not go and it was pointed out where we would be going once we progressed from week one. Somehow I imagined that everyone would get through week one. *How wrong could I be?*

During the afternoon we were escorted to the Ship's barbers. Here, each new rating took a turn in the barber's chair. One guy, who had particularly long shoulder length hair, was the first invitee.

The barber smiled and asked, "How would you like your hair cut sir?"

"Only a slight trim," replied the naive recruit smiling back at the barber.

At that, the guy's full head of hair fell to the floor. So shocked and horrified was the guy that he ran out of the barber's shop crying. I understand that he left HMS Raleigh within two hours of his barber's chair encounter.

Later we were sent for medical checks. We were herded into a Nissan hut that had an adjoining door to another Nissan hut. Nissan Huts were buildings made of corrugated sheeting and which resembled a large arch. Each Nissan hut could hold about 50 people seated. We were instructed to strip naked and to stand in line facing the adjoining door. In turn, we went through the door to be greeted by the ship's doctor and two male nurses. We had our temperatures and blood pressures checked, were examined thoroughly all over, had to do several pull-ups on a metal overhead bar and at the same time had our testicles felt while having to cough. We were made to bend over and told to spread our bum cheeks. One of the nurses then examined the entrance to our anus. I'm still not sure whether they were checking for haemorrhoids, lost property, or evidence of previous entry or whether or not we had wiped our arses clean. Once the examination was completed, we exited the building from another door to the outside and made to walk back to the point of entry where we were allowed to dress. I remember the day being quite warm and sunny and was glad of it. The thought of walking out in cold, windy or rainy weather would have been daunting. How glad was I that I was a May recruit and not part of the winter intake.

After dinner we all set about trying to learn the knowledge provided within the two books we had been given. POME Lewis told us to make sure that we understood the rules and regulations and provided us with lengths of rope so that we could try to tie the multitude of knots found on the pages of the seaman's manual.

At 20:42 precisely, we heard for the first time, *Sunset.*

Sunset is played at sunset in every naval establishment throughout the world and on some ships. Where it is not played, a call is given using a bosons' call (type of whistle) and the Royal Ensign (British Naval Flag) is lowered. The origin of this ceremony is obscure, but according to Royal Marine factsheets, there is no doubt that it was one of the earliest to be instituted. One of the first references appears to have been made to such a ceremony, which was then called 'Watch Setting', in the *Rules and Ordynaunces for the Warre*, dated 1554, and also by Robert Barrett in his *Theorike and Practice of Moderne Warres*, dated 1598. It appears that the original 'call' was beaten by drums alone, and that it was some years before fifes were introduced. The bugle came at a later date still, and the present ceremony of having a band paraded is a modern innovation, which is purely used as a spectacle. In olden times, when the hours of darkness meant a cessation of hostilities until the following day, the object of the call was to collect and post the necessary guards for the camp, for the night. It was also a warning for those outside the camp to return or they would be kept outside for the night.

There is some confusion arising between 'Retreat' and 'Tattoo', but this confusion may, in part, have been caused owing to the French using the word 'Retraite' for the familiar call to our 'Tattoo'. From extracts from old orders, it would appear conclusive that retreat was meant to be separate from tattoo and to be beaten at sunset. From the first time of hearing *Sunset* until now, I always get a lump in my throat when hearing *Sunset* being played.

At 9:00 pm each and every night, we were provided with hot drinks and a snack. This included sandwiches, cake, biscuits or cheese and crackers. These snacks are known as 'Nineoclockers' and are a firm favourite with all serving matelot's. After gorging on these tasty morsels, it was time for the nightly bed routine of preparing clothes for the next day and showering before bed and lights out.

Our second full day and third day in New Entry was the actual day of signing up for service. After breakfast, we mustered in the meeting room and were told what signing up actually meant. Today we would be marched in front of the duty officer, be asked if we understood the consequences of joining Her Majesty's forces and that we understood the rules and obligations of service. We were also informed that this would be our last day of being a civilian and that if we had any doubts whatsoever, we should not sign the committal documents or sign the Official Secrets Act to which we must comply. Several guys left at this point realising that this was no game and that once they had signed, they would not be able to change their mind.

Those that were left, lined up, were marched forward individually and invited to sign both documents. This was quite a solemn event and the enormity of the

17

occasion didn't quite hit home until months after. On signing up, we were then given our ID number, a number that is engrained into my being to this day. D116406(W), JME (M), [Junior Marine Engineer (Mechanic)] Tuckley. Later the postfix of 'W' was added to the number. I am not sure why this letter was added or what it referred to. Later, and a further 'M' (Mechanic) added to the JME. The letter 'D' identified to which Naval Dockyard you were assigned to; 'D' being Devonport and 'P' was given to those who were assigned to Portsmouth.

Following the declaration of intent, those of us who had signed were taken to have photographs taken. This was akin to being arrested. We had to write our ID number on a short chalk board and hold it chest high for frontal and sideways portraits. Our photographs were processed and one was taken to be sealed on our official ID card. The others were for Naval records and one for our passports, which we received just prior to deployment on our first ship or, if travelling abroad for other reasons.

The afternoon was taken up in collecting our uniforms from the Quarter Master's Store. We were measured and issued with our number one and two uniforms; tropical uniforms; hats; white fronts; collars; silks; lanyards; boots (ceremonial and everyday wear); shoes (black and white); sandals; number eights (working uniforms); woollies (jumpers); overalls; sports gear, including tops, shorts, socks and plimsolls; badges for all uniforms, including gold braid for number one's, red for number two's and white and blue for tropical and working uniforms; shoe brushes and cleaning polish; belts; spats; cap ribbons; a sewing kit and a wooden block with our name in raised letter, that were to be used for marking each and every item of kit.

The evening was spent printing name tags and sewing these onto overalls and number eight's. Badges were sewn on to respective uniforms and cap ribbons tied with the appropriate bow to the right hand side of the hats. By 8:00 pm, we were fully kitted out and a demonstration of how to iron each item was given by POME Lewis. The hat ribbons and bow had to be pressed, number eight's ironed and pressed ready for the following day; collars had to have obligatory two tits and a fanny crease (two convex and one concave) pressed in so as it could be folded precisely to be stored and seven creases had to be pressed into a concertina for number one and two trousers. Possibly the most difficult to fold, iron and press was the 'silk'. The silk is a black piece of fabric approximately a foot wide and two and a half foot long. The silk had to be folded lengthwise until it measured only one inch, and then twisted once before each end is sewn together. The following day would be the day when we wore any part of our uniform for the very first time.

The following morning after reveille (reveille is played as a bugle call to signal the beginning of the duty day on base) and showering, we put on our number eight uniform as instructed and were lined up outside. From here on in, we would march everywhere. Walking was not permitted. Just going for breakfast was the proudest day of my life. Head up, shoulders back, swinging arms and looking great in my uniform. I had the biggest grin ever. Pugh and I marched side by side and although we were to 'Keep eyes front', we occasionally glanced at each other smiling. Pugh and I laughed as some of the guys could not march. They were what we called 'tick-tocking'. Tick-tocking is when the arm moves in the same direction as the leg on either side, similar to walking like a robot.

Our fourth day was devoted to and spending time learning how to wash, and press other parts of our uniform; how to polish boots and shoes; how to store all items of uniform and civilian gear in the small locker provided and how to present uniforms for inspection at kit musters. I found to my amusement that the seaman's manual was not only there to provide information of basic ships husbandry, but also doubled as a size guide for making sure every item of clothing was exact in size for presentation at kit musters. A pictorial layout of how kit was to be presented for muster was given on the first page of the Seamen's manual. We spent three hours just ironing the toecap of our boots with a hot spoon, then melting black shoe polish to 'bully' the toecap to a mirror shine. This wasn't as easy as it sounds because each toecap had raised pimple-like structures which had to be flattened before you could apply polish; the same for shoes too. Why the manufacturers couldn't use smooth leather on toecaps was beyond me, but I suppose that raised pimple leather is cheaper than flat smooth leather.

Learning to clean to Navy standards is hard. Everything, and I mean everything, has to be cleaned to an exact standard. There was no new-fangled cleaning equipment, no vacuum cleaners; no electric floor buffers; no washing machines; tumble dryers, nothing. The key to cleaning in the Royal Navy is 'elbow grease'. For some reason, the Navy has a fetish for brass and shiny aluminium. The brass cleaning fluid was called 'Bluebell'. We must have used at least ten tins of the stuff per week. Bluebell also doubled up as a drinking spirit, which I found out much later in my career. Because drinking on board HMS ships is limited to three cans of beer per day for ratings. The chance to get extra rations was always a talking point in every mess, whether on board ship or naval base. Bluebell could be strained through bread to produce a foul tasting and smelly clear liquid, but diluted with coke produced quite a kick. I expect it eventually rotted the liver but the internal organs must have shined. At this time, 'grog' was also on ration. Grog was a type of thick rum made from molasses and given to all ratings on a daily basis watered down to make it palatable. The history of giving grog to rating dated back over 300 years but sadly ended in the morning of 31 July 1970, due to the ever increasing sophistication of weaponry on board ships and the fear that a drunken sailor might blow him and the ship out of the water. Grog and beer would be traded between ratings as barter. Given the amount of cleaning one had to do, some non-drinkers would happily trade their beer, grog and Bluebell to those who craved alcohol in exchange for a cleaning duty. Polishing, scrubbing, mopping, wiping and keeping the place 'Ship Shape' was a daily occurrence and from this first week in New Entry, I remain obsessed with cleaning.

Our fifth day saw us raw recruits practicing marching skills. Drill from this point was a daily activity (I have to say that I am so pleased, as a child and young man in civilian life, I had always been part of organisations where marching had been the norm). From cubs' scouts, boys' brigade and army cadets, the skill of marching was instilled. For me, marching was a natural, for others the pain of being shouted at and humiliated often became too much to bear. Two guys in particular suffered most. Both would 'Tick-tock', swinging the arms in the same direction as their leg movement rather than having the arms swinging in the opposite direction to leg movement. They also had difficulty in knowing their left from their right, often falling into the ranks knocking others over as they attempted to turn in the wrong direction from the main body of the group.

Our afternoon was then spent at the 'Oral Butchers' or dentist as most of you call them. Navel dentists at the point of entry were absolute butchers. I had a front tooth missing on entry to the Royal Navy from an accident which occurred in the school playground when I was nine years old. Apart from the missing tooth, I reckon that I had a really sound set of gnashers. Week one in New Entry soon changed that. From henceforth until the completion of my basis training, I attended the oral butchers on a weekly basis and had every tooth in my head filled in some shape or form. Not only did I have every tooth filled, every other rating in my intake also had the same. That's 32 teeth times' 90 recruits, equalling 2,880 fillings. I swore there was more metal in the average sailor's mouth than there were rivets in a World War II battleship.

School time represented the rest of the day. Classroom based learning was regular and intense. All ratings had to be fully literate and numerate, attaining levels of competency equivalent to A' levels. All rating had to pass their Maths and English to progress. By the end of this first week, the number ready for progression had reduced considerably. Some never made it past the first week because they could not meet the demanding standards set both in educational terms and in achieving assessed goals in marching, cleaning and personal hygiene.

Saturday gave rise to more marching and during the afternoon, sports. We were taken in the afternoon to the gymnasium where we were pushed to our limits by Naval PTIs (Physical Training Instructors). Circuit training, core body training, strength-based training, cardio-vascular training, you name it we did it. It was exhausting. I saw myself as being relatively fit but this session was even above any standard that I had ever done. Following the training session, we had to set up the gym with every available piece of equipment available in the gym to play a game called 'Pirates'. This game saw one team chasing another with the purpose of retrieving a coloured belt attached to the back of the opposing team. Also, none of the participants were allowed to place their feet on the gymnasium floor, so we had to manoeuvre around balancing on the equipment available. The game was brutal. Several of the guys ended up with significant bruises, cuts, grazes, sprains and abrasions. "Get over it," was the rallying cry from the PTIs and "Stop being a Woos" to anyone complaining of injury.

Following gym, we were taken to the swimming pool. Three hours of gym had taken its toll, now for swimming. I loved swimming and was very proficient. I loved the whole experience of relaxing in the water and covering 50 lengths. Others struggled, some really badly and it was clear that some had a fear of water. I remember thinking, *fancy joining the Navy when you can't swim*, to me it seemed such a stupid thing to do, why not join the RAF or Army? Little did I know that some guys had not volunteered to join the Navy but were 'Press Ganged' by Magistrates, join or go to Borstal, learn to swim!

Saturday evening was given to kit cleaning. We were not even allowed to go to the NAFFE during our first week and all of us were desperate to have some form of respite. Sunday morning gave us the respite we were looking for, Church

Parade. Sunday was the first time that we had worn number ones (Parade Uniform). It took quite a while to actually figure out how to dress properly in our uniforms, especially putting on the collars, silks, ribbons and lanyards but once on, wow, did we look and feel good. The sense of pride was overwhelming and even though we marched like a rabble, no one could detract from this feeling of self-importance. At church, we were split into denominations, Catholic, CofE, Presbyterian and non-believers. Each group was then marched into their respective places of worship and the non-believers were taken to the Parade Ground for an hour of Drill. The whole camp attended Church Parade and there were hundreds of sailors, artificers, non-commissioned officers and officers all looking splendid and well turned out. A Company of Royal Marine Commandos were also present, immaculately turned out and the band resplendent. It felt as if we were at a Military Tattoo, undesirable from the inside but so utterly powerful and patriotic looking from the outside. An overwhelming sense of belonging swept over me and I still have that same feeling of belonging to the navy to this very day.

Following Church Service, our Division, led by POME. Lewis had the obligatory official black and white photograph taken. Each new entry division had an official photograph and each of us was presented with a copy several days later. Our afternoon was taken up packing all of our gear into the holdall and suitcase provided by the navy ready for the move from New Entry to our new home in Basis Training. The Nissan Huts for Basis Training were at the opposite side of the camp to New Entry, but this move represented a major step towards deployment and towards being deployed to our first ships.

Chapter Two
Basic Training

The start of our ten week basic training began by allocating all of the New Recruits to their respective divisions. I was placed in Eagle Division and others to the other four divisions; Frobisher, Collingwood, Leander and Hawk. Our division was led by the Divisional Lieutenant (DO), a Chief Petty Officer (CPO) and a Petty Officer (PO). We were housed in a corrugated Nissan hut comprising of ten beds, ten lockers and a table with ten chairs. The heads (toilets), showers and dobby area (place to do your washing and ironing) was situated at the back of the hut. Beside each bed was a metal framed window which opened onto a grassed area between each Nissan hut and a view to the next Nissan hut. After being allocated our bed space, we were given time to unpack and get our lockers in order. Our next task was to meet with the divisional team. There was one Nissan hut allocated for divisional meetings and we were all shepherded into the divisional mess hall to find out what was expected of us over the next ten weeks and what our fates would be. We were encouraged to sit on the floor around the divisional mess hall where our divisional Petty Officer made his introductions. POME Wann was a rather large, burly, middle-aged guy who wore a full set (beard). The wearing of beards was only allowed by formal request and the wearer must be able to grow enough facial hair to ensure a solid covering of the top lip and chin. The beard had to be trimmed neatly and must be linked to straight sideburns. Moustaches alone were not allowed; they were only allowed for those in the army or Royal Air Force. POME Wann, a Glaswegian had been in the Royal Navy for almost 20 years but had held on to his almost incoherent accent. During his introduction, one guy whispered something to a guy sitting next to him.

POME Wann's hearing was acute; he immediately eyed the guy booming, "Hey yous, whats ya fucking name?"

The guy responded sheepishly giving his surname.

"What's ya fucking number?"

Jones tried to respond but found it difficult to remember and mumbled nervously.

"Ye canna remember ya fucking number Jones and ya interrupt me when I'm talkin', ya fuckin Sassenach. Yous do that agen lad and yall git a fuckin' kick a ya lamps." (Apparently, 'lamps' referred to testicles, a term that I had never heard before.)

There was complete and utter silence, a few smiles but the majority were near shitting themselves. POME Wann made sure that we understood that no one should talk unless spoken to and that 'childlike behaviour' stopped here.

At that moment, the Chief Petty Officer arrived at the door from an adjacent office followed behind by the divisional officer. POME Wann immediately sprung to attention, ordered us all on to our feet, called us to attention and the CPO (Chief) and DO entered the room.

"All ratings ready for your inspection sir," shouted POME Wann.

"Thank you POME Wann. As you were," replied the DO.

POME Wann then instructed us all to sit down again so that the DO could begin his introductory speech. He stood looking smart in his Officers' Uniform with his two gold rings shinning on his jacket wrists. He held in his right hand his ceremonial sword but had a face that looked as if he had just been defeated in a boxing ring. He had piggy eyes, a bloated, ruddy complexion and lips and nose of an over enthusiastic Botox user. Our DO was not the most pleasant man on earth as we were to find out over the next ten weeks. In fact, he had a real sadistic nature and his ceremonial sword was just one tool in his dominatrix wooden chest. CPO Giddings on the other hand was a real gentleman, having been in the Royal Navy for 18 years, had climbed up the ladder to reach the highest non-commissioned officer rank. Chief Petty Officer Giddings had really kind eyes and a warm smile. He was a Brummie, and I just knew that we would get on well.

The DO set out his set of rules; these were not all compulsory Naval rules, others were his own rules and went far beyond those required under navy regulation. The DO wanted his division to come out on top and anything less than your very best was still not going to be good enough for him. The DO was a disciplinarian, authoritative and dictatorial. From day one, the division had named him 'Mengele', after that notorious angel of death in Hitler's death squad.

He reiterated that over the next ten weeks, we could expect an action-packed and challenging time and that we would be expected to act and behave as a team. Anyone not making the grade could expect action being taken against him and the possibility of being 'kicked out' of the navy. The DO then handed over to Chief Giddings before leaving the divisional mess hall.

Chief Giddings, after saluting the DO turned towards us and the minute the DO had gone, the room appeared to relax somewhat, but still, everyone was attentive. Chief Giddings informed us that our training would enable each and every one of us to develop core values that were essential to the Royal Navy and that by the end of our training, each person would willingly give his life for one of his opposite numbers (our fellow ratings), Chief Giddings informed us that not everyone would complete their basic training and only the 'Crème de la crème' would achieve to warrant 'Passing Out' from training. We were told that we had to develop commitment, and respect and that through discipline, we would then be able to prove our integrity, loyalty and through courage would become a true representative of Her Majesties' forces. We would learn basic skills of self-discipline and teamwork. We would have to overcome problems, both on a personal level but also to ensure the safety and well-being of our ship mates. Chief Giddings opening remarks were inspiring and motivating, he gave everyone a sense of achievement, even before we had actually achieved anything. Chief Giddings was someone that we all wanted to aspire to be like.

During the ten weeks of basic training, we had numerous kit musters. Having to clean, press and present our kit for inspection by the PO and CPO on a daily basis, to the DO on a weekly basis, and to the Captain on a three-week basis; these were known as 'Rounds'. This also included the full cleaning of the mess and adjoining rooms. Being criticised by others for very minor mistakes was bad enough but to be totally humiliated, demoralised and soul destroyed was at another level. Not only did we have to show improvements in how we maintained our kit, we also had to show how we had developed in other skills. We had to be as precise as a brain surgeon and meet exacting standards. I recall the hours we spent at those Belfast sinks, scrubbing our whites to ensure that there was not a blemish. Our fingers would often crack and bleed to ensure that dirt and mud had been removed from working uniforms, overalls and sports equipment. We were provided with a scrubbing brush and a bar of carbolic soap, known as 'Pusser's hard'. Actual washing powder was not provided. This we had to purchase from the camp NAFFI. Payday was every two weeks and as none of us had yet received any pay we were reliant on pusser's hard for the first week in basic training. The hours we spent ironing and pressing, ensuring that each crease was as sharp as a razor, each crease matching exactly, and was in line with other creases in collars and trousers, was endless. Measuring clothes to ensure kit was the exact size became an art. We would work well into the early hours to ensure that we got a good review, but it never happened.

DO kit musters were the hardest to endure. When we had daily rounds, the only response from the PO and CO would be a shouting at close quarters telling us just how useless we were and occasionally we had clothes and footwear thrown across the mess. At DO kit musters, all windows in our Nissan hut had to be opened fully before inspection of our kit took place and outside, on the grassed area, we had to ensure that it had been well watered. The watering of the grassed area was always done by a rating from another division who was given this task as punishment for some slight mistake he had made. The DO would ensure that some or all of our kit was thrown out of the window at each kit muster ensuring that it landed firmly in the worst part of the quagmire. If any rating had an exceptionally bad muster, his bed and bedding followed his kit through the window. The most severe punishment for the worst presented kit muster would then be to go outside and commence jumping on his kit and bedding to make sure that mud became ingrained. We would then be ordered to have another kit muster the following day and each day until the DO was satisfied. If you have never seen men cry, then this would be the place to see it happen. Frustration, anger and tiredness took its toll and of course, we were not allowed to show any weakness, holding back our boiling annoyance and fury became a well-developed skill.

Drill was the second most important activity. Not only did POME Wann have us marching up and down the hill outside our mess at every opportunity but we also had drill on the parade ground on a daily basis, firstly getting everyone to march in time and in line, and then learning manoeuvres, turning, wheeling, reversing, about turning, moving on the diagonal, dressing in quick time, double quick time and slow time, first without rifles, then with rifles and then finally with rifles with fixed bayonets. The art of marching with rifles with fixed bayonets led on to shouldering and presenting arms. The Navy's weapon of choice at that time was the SLR (Self Loading Rifle). Once, when dressing with rifles, we were ordered 'eyes right'; our heads turning sharply to the right whilst at same time our left arms swung up to reach the shoulder of the person to our left. This provided distancing and enabled us to see if the line was straight. Having rifles with fixed bayonets meant that you had to pull the barrel of the rifle close into the shoulder. The weight of the rifle had a habit of moving forward leaving the bayonet sticking out in a forward position. On more than one occasion, some poor bloke caught his hand on his opposite number's bayonet. We were ordered to eyes front, a manoeuvre which saw everyone turn their eyes sharply to the front and pulling their left arm down at your side, at speed. If someone caught their hand on their opposite number's bayonet, the person bleeding was ordered not to bleed on the parade ground. Our Gunnery Officer hated the sight of blood on his parade ground and in the event of any accidents, the poor patient, after attending sick bay, would have to return to scrub the ground to remove any unsightly marks. Should any of ratings not meet the Gunnery Officer's exact standards, we would have to continue marching after the main body of the group had been sent away for their break. On occasion, the Gunnery Officer would make the poor sod return, once our duty was complete, to undergo extracurricular activity, this could include cutting the grass around the perimeter of the parade ground with scissors, or having the coal next to the boiler house painted white. We marched everywhere, never walking, never running (except when ordered to do so) and absolutely no slouching. Shoulders back, stomach in, chest out was shouted more times than I can remember. In addition to marching with rifles, we were also taught how to fire the SLR assault rifle, as well as SMGs (Sub machine guns) and hand pistols. The firing of arms accurately is a skill required of all sailors. I was quite good at firing arms and managed to hit the targets quite accurately. Some however, tended to close their eyes at the point of pulling the trigger. This is a natural reaction to the noise that the guns give off. Overcoming this natural reaction takes time and practice but even so, one or two of the guys still could not hit the target.

Basic training was nearly all practical. We had to carryout team activities and undergo team events to show how well we could work together. Training at locations like Pier Cellars and Dartmoor provided great outdoor adventures with key purposes. Pier Cellars is used by HMS Raleigh as an assault course and training base, this hidden away historical site was once used for the development and testing of torpedoes. Out-of-bounds to the public, with a chained metal gate warning passers-by that the site is owned and protected by the MoD (Ministry of Defence), Pier Cellars, a former Elizabethan Pilchard Harbour, is now used by the HMS Raleigh naval base for a 28-hour exercise, known as 'Daring Leap'.

This exercise is carried out during week four of the recruits' ten-week initial naval training course. The visit to Pier Cellars is the first time new entry recruits leave HMS Raleigh from their date of joining. Over the course, recruits have to complete an 8.7 km navigation exercise around the Rame peninsula. There are 15 checkpoints and we were made to carry our Bergen's (Rucksacks), which weighed approximately ten kg. This prepares us for a longer navigation exercise on Dartmoor during week seven. At Pier Cellars, we were made to complete teambuilding exercises including raft building, then had to transport equipment across the harbour on the 'Jacob's ladder' (a Jacob's ladder consists of blocks of wood held together by strings or ribbons). We built our rafts from plastic containers, pieces of wood and nylon rope and then 'sailed' them across the harbour to rescue our instructor. In addition, we took part in physical training exercises and played an activity called 'superstars'. 'Superstars' was a competition between divisions. We ran an assault course, swam across the bay, lifted and carried logs and flipped tyres, built camps and learned survival techniques. Each exercise was given points and by the end of our 28 hours, one division was crowned the winner. This was not just dependent upon which team came first, but on how well the teams worked as a cohesive group.

There was also an assault course within the grounds of HMS Raleigh. Like all assault courses, there are always ropes and water involved. HMS Raleigh's assault course had a single rope bridge that stretched over what we were told was a cess pit (effluent water coming from one of the barracks). I'm not sure if this was actually true or not but it certainly made us very aware that it would be very unpleasant to fall in. As you can imagine, everyone fell off the rope at some point and for those who almost made it across the rope bridge, there was always an instructor at each end of the rope who ensured that you fell off. The water stunk and there was about two foot of slime at the bottom. We practiced weekly to improve our time and technique to master this course and it became obvious that our team working skills gradually improved to make sure everyone got over the course in double quick time.

Wednesday afternoons was dedicated to inter-divisional sports. Before we all met at the various sports venues, we were mustered in the Divisional mess meeting room where we were given the opportunity to choose the sport we would like to participate in. I was an excellent swimmer and was fast, probably one of the faster swimmers of this intake. I have been swimming since I was three and took to water like a duck. Because of my ability, I was always put forward for swimming, as our DO wanted our division to be top of the league. The DO would also come in to the Divisional meeting mess armed with a cricket bat and a broken oar. These were not equipment to be used for any of the sports but were his intimidation tools. The DO would stand in front of each rating asking what sport he would like to be involved in that day. Each rating would then state their preferred sport. If the DO did not want you to participate in your chosen sport, he would hit you on top of the head with either the cricket bat or oar. He would then ask again what sport you wanted to participate in. You would be hit on the head until you got the sport that he wanted you to be involved with. One week, I wanted to participate in a cross-country run (another sport I excelled in), not happy with my reply, I was bashed on the head with a cricket bat until I chose swimming. Another of the DO's favourite pass times was to check haircuts. Ratings were not allowed to grow sideburns unless they were full, straight and could reach to the bottom of the earlobe. All sideburns, including those that did not reach the top of the earlobe had to be straight. The DO took our Wednesday meeting to check that everyone's hair met regulations. If anyone was found to have facial hair where it shouldn't be, the DO would take out his sword and with the tip, took delight in shaving the excess hair off the offender. He was particularly good at shaving around the left ear with his sword and invariably nicked the ratings ear causing it to bleed. I am sure that there are many a rating that had been in this division who are now walking about with only half a left ear.

Discipline was swift and hard. Any misdemeanours were dealt with harshly. I was given a daily job of cleaning the DO's office. Many a time, I was told to wait outside while a rating was reprimanded. Several ratings were discharged from the navy during basic training; some for sexual inappropriate behaviour, some for continual poor hygiene, some for theft, and some for breaking regulations or because they were not making the grade. Some were not dealt with by the DO but were put on a charge and had to appear before the Captain. This was known as Captain's Table. Funny enough, those who went to Captain's Table either never returned or would be put back several weeks. For those put back, their basic training lasted much longer than the ten weeks allocated.

One evening while cleaning our mess, it was decided that two beds would be dismantled and made up to look as if nothing had been done to them. The two beds belonged to two guys who had serious hygiene problems. To try to persuade them to improve their hygiene, they were taken to the shower block and scrubbed with Vim (an abrasive cleaning powder) and long handled deck scrubber. They were scrubbed so hard that each bled. The reason for this harsh treatment was because the whole mess would be punished for the crimes of the few and poor hygiene was seen as a crime. After showering the offenders, they were left to get ready for bed. As they got into bed, their beds collapsed. The whole mess thought this was highly amusing and began laughing and wailing. The noise was so loud that it drew the attention of the duty officer, who came into the mess shouting and asking what the hell was going on. We were made to muster outside, in pyjamas, in the pouring rain and explain what had happened. We were left outside for an hour to reflect on the stupidity of our actions and warned that with the dawn there would be repercussions for our childish behaviour. The following morning, the DO came into the mess in a foul mood. He understood why the scrubbing of our opposite numbers was carried out but could not see the funny side of the dismantling of the beds. His response was to make us do the 'Bed race'.

The divisional mess rooms were built during the 1950s and were large, basic corrugated Nissan huts each housing 10–15 ratings. There were approximately nine Nissan huts on each side of a road that was built on a fairly steep hill. The bed race took place on this hill. Outside of the top Nissan hut, were placed four beds, two standing horizontal to the road and two facing vertical to the road. About one third and at about two thirds down the road were two more beds horizontally placed and two more at the bottom of the hill. Ratings from our mess were gathered at the top of the hill and split into two teams. Two ratings from each team had to dismantle the two vertical beds, push them under the horizontal bed, and reassemble the bed. Once reassembled, the two ratings had to run to the next bed, disassemble the bed they were carrying, push the bed under the horizontals and reassemble again, repeating when they reached the bottom, then repeat again and race back to the top, dismantling and reassembling each time. When at the top, the next two ratings had to take over and so forth until all the ratings had completed a run. On the running stage and to make things more difficult, the DO and POME Wann got on to one of the beds that had to be carried. At the same time, as they were being carried, they beat each rating on the head with rowing oars, swinging in an overhead pendulum motion as to maintain consistency. By the end of the run, all those running were totally exhausted, were well-battered and bruised; some had attained head injuries and had to report to sick bay to have cuts on their heads stitched. It was very clear to us all, that any type of pranks using naval equipment would be punished in an appropriate manner and would include the equipment within the punishment regime.

This had been the first time any of us had run up and down this hill but very quickly we became accustomed to it, as the hill was used as a punishment for any minor offence. One time, the mess were made to run up and down the hill for three hours, in full sun and on one of the hottest days of the year. Several of us were eventually carted off to sickbay with heat exhaustion.

Our divisional officer was notorious for his bullying tactics and sadistic nature. One guy who had survived his basic training and had passed out, had then gone on to become a Royal Naval Nurse. The guy returned to Raleigh to serve as a member of Raleigh's ships company. His hatred of our DO landed him in serious trouble after our DO visited the sickbay for a minor ailment. On meeting the nurse, our DO was taken into an examination room and instructed to strip off. He was then told to bend over the examination table to have his temperature taken. He was informed that only anal thermometers were available. The DO followed the orders given by the nurse who then inserted a dull cold implement into the DO's anus and then left the room.

After ten minutes, the door to the examination room opened and the Chief Medical Officer (DMO) asked the DO, "What are you doing lieutenant?"

"I'm having my temperature taken," replied the DO.

"What!" cried the medical officer. "With a daffodil?"

The nurse apparently had seen an opportunity to humiliate the DO but paid the consequences with a court martial. The image of the DO bent over an examination table with a daffodil stuck up his arse still brings a smile to my face.

Each week we also had to take part in boxing. During the last week of basic training we were expected to fight a full bout, 'six times three' minute rounds. This became one of the highlights of basic training which all recruits attended. The noise in the sports hall was tremendous. The room was testosterone filled and by the end of the session blood from numerous noses, eyebrows and lips was splashed on the canvas. The boxing bout was not a measure of how well young men could fight but was a measure of stamina and to see whether each rating would be prepared to hold his own over a period of time when the situation became a little tough.

Another part of basic training consisted of firefighting and damage control training. All ratings had to gain knowledge of this at a basic level in case situations that might be presented on board ship. We learned how to deal with a variety of fires including oil fires, electrical fires and gas fires and where combustible goods caught fire through explosion. From classroom based learning we moved to practical training, dealing individually with fires and tackling large fires as a team. We were made to work in smoke filled compartments using breathing apparatus and recover bodies. The realism was quite astonishing, even the dummies were lifelike, weighing the same as an average man.

Damage control was also carried out in the same fashion. For damage control, we were placed within a simulator which replicated part of a ship. Once in the simulator, doors were locked and the simulator would shift in a variety of directions as might happen in rough seas. The simulator was then flooded and our task was to stem the water from entering the simulator compartment. Power to the simulator was also cut off. We had to work in the dark or with restricted lighting and much of the work was done through touch. Wooden wedges, fire blankets and bedding had been place within the simulator and we worked hard hammering in the wooden wedges and stuffing in the blankets with anything available, while at the same time, more water came flooding in. We were able to reduce some of the water flow by turning off valves and shutting bulkhead doors. We also had to address gashes that had been made in the structure and which represented damage to the framework of the ship. Much damage can be caused through collision, running aground and from damage caused during fighting in wartime situations. Our basic training enabled all ratings to act but more specialised training was given at a later stage to those who worked in engineering. As a marine engineer, I along with others who were to become marine engineers would have to undertake a greater responsibility in firefighting and damage control because the possibility of fires within our work areas was far greater than anywhere else on a ship apart from on flight decks.

During the early 1970s, Britain along with their NATO allies were at the height of the Cold War with Russia. The threat of a possible war with Russia was never far from everyone's thoughts. Nuclear, Biological and Chemical, Defence (NBCD) was core to our training, particularly after the threat of nuclear action when Russia threatened to place nuclear warheads on Cuba. Classroom education on all aspects of NBCD was covered thoroughly but even with this education, we quickly realised that should there be a nuclear strike, many of us would not survive.

We also had to pass a first aid course. We were taught through a mixture of both practical and theory. We were instructed on how to examine a casualty, use a defibrillator, familiarise ourselves with basic life support and learned how to control bleeding and trauma. These provide the skills to overcome a potentially threatening situation long enough for medically trained individuals to arrive on scene. Other essential first aid skills are taught such as treating burns and scalds as well as assisting a choking individual.

On week seven, we were taken to Dartmoor where we had to take part in an overnight forced march. We gathered at Prince Town having been transported there by truck. This was an early start and we had to be up and ready by 04:30 am. When we arrived in Prince Town, we were given maps to aid our travel across country. The aim was to meet at a fixed point some 22 miles away and to find our way through a variety of terrains and checkpoints. Dartmoor is a bleak place at night and the going can get very tough. Not only are you going on hard ground, down valleys and up hills, there are also rock formations to be climbed, bog marshes to cross and the ever-changing weather conditions to contend with.

Our night on Dartmoor occurred on possibly the wettest night of the year. We had torrential rain, fog and poor visibility to contend with. Groups of six were sent off at 20-minute intervals. The first few miles were not too bad apart from having the driving rain in your face, drenching all of your clothes as well as the kit you had to carry. We managed to arrive at the checkpoints on time and managed the rough terrain well, albeit our feet were cold and wet. When we arrived at the bog marsh, it was evident that no one could walk through it, as each person began to sink knee-deep in the thick, mossy mud. The only way across was to lie flat and crawl. Lying flat enabled the body weight to be distributed evenly and enabled you to use both arms and legs to push yourself forward. By the end of the crawl, our clothes and kit had accumulated much more water and mud, making it harder to walk. As we marched, we saw the outline of Dartmoor prison in the distance. I recall thinking just how remote this prison was from civilisation and how demoralising it must feel for those who had been taken there to serve their sentences. Near to exhaustion and with daylight breaking, we saw the endpoint. The last mile or so had to be covered by road. Our team leader encouraged us all to make a valiant effort and to run the last few hundred yards but with feet being cold and sore, this effort was purgatory. Our group made it just in time and our efforts were rewarded by being told that we would not have to do this exercise again. Our second reward was a drink of hot chocolate and a sandwich, before being piled back onto awaiting trucks to return to Raleigh. Some groups did not make the run within the given time frame and had to return to Dartmoor later that week to take a re-run. Getting cleaned up took an age but we celebrated by standing in hot showers fully clothed just to get warm. After about half an hour, we gradually stripped off to wash. I recall that it took most of the day to fully wash, then clean, dry and press all of our gear ready for the following day's kit muster. Although still very tired the next morning, we all found a sense of pride in our achievement.

At the end of our ten-week basic training came the 'Passing Out' Parade. Those who had successfully completed their basic training would parade in front of Officers, Naval dignitary and the families of those passing out. My mother and sister-in-law had travelled down from the Midlands to witness this event. We marched and presented as a guard of honour, carried out a variety of manoeuvres, were led by the Royal Marine band and listened to speeches given by the commanding officer; after which, we were allowed to meet our families and we were encouraged to give our families a tour of HMS Raleigh. This was followed by lunch, which was far better than the food served every day in the galley. My sister-in-law had with her one of my nephews, who was about a year old. He attracted more attention than the parade. The CPO of my division was interested in meeting my family as they had so much in common in terms of the area in which they had come from. My CPO agreed that when he was next in the Midlands, he would call on my family for a social visit.

Only eleven weeks into my service I could already feel a change in me. My mother also sensed this change and looked upon me in a different way than she had when I was at home. Many would say that there was a maturity about me and I guess that I noticed this too. Being in the armed services certainly changes individuals very quickly, far quicker than anything which might happen in civilian life.

The following week we were given two weeks leave. We were issued with travel warrants and told that when we were out, we must wear uniform. I believe that we were probably the last intake of recruits to follow this rule as all armed forces personal were put on high alert because of attacks that had taken place by those opposed to those defending their country. In Britain, at that time, the IRA had begun to take to the offensive and conducted a relatively high-intensity campaign against the British and Northern Ireland security forces and the infrastructure of the state. These activities by the IRA were beginning to happen on the main land of Great Britain as well as in Northern Island.

Going home for the first time was actually quite strange. People would walk up and touch my naval collar. This was seen by the older generation as a sign that would bring good luck or good fortune. Everyone appeared more interested in me as an individual just because I was in uniform. When going out to pubs for a drink with my brothers, people would buy me drinks, even though I had never met them before. It was as if I had been placed on a pedestal. The respect I gained from adults and particularly older adults was immense.

Younger youths also saw my uniform as a sign to see how tough I really was and wanting to fight or provoke arguments to test this out. *What is it with people's mentality?* I could not get my head around it and longed to be back in the security of Raleigh. Returning to Raleigh was invigorating. No longer was I a New Entry on Basic Training, I was now going into specialist training and therefore treated differently when walking around the base.

Not all of our time at Raleigh was work and learning, although most of the time we were. We often spent our evenings in the NAAFI (Navy, Army, Air Force Institutes), where we could at least get a drink (albeit we were not supposed to drink underage, we still were able to buy beer), play pool, darts, skittles and listen to music. We also had shore leave, which allowed us to occasionally go to explore Plymouth. I was lucky in the fact that CPO Giddings had befriended me and had asked if I could 'babysit' for him whilst he and his wife went out some evenings. Because of this, other non-commissioned officers also employed me to do the same for them, including the Padre. I was making extra money doing this and it did give me a chance to get away and enjoy some sort of home life. Always supplied with drinks and chocolate and getting money was a great incentive and also having the luxury of sitting watching television without interruption, was bliss.

Before I commenced my specialist training, I also had several days where I was not expected to work. CPO Giddings allowed me to stay at his house, where I became friends with his eldest son. Those days were spent on the beach or just visiting monuments that are strewn throughout Plymouth. On one occasion, I also stayed at Aggie Weston's (The Royal Sailors Rest). There were two such establishments in Plymouth and one in Portsmouth, these establishments offer a place for Royal Navy personnel to meet, have decent food and where they could 'bed down' for the night. Agnes Weston was a member of the Christian

Temperance movement during the 1800s who corresponded with sailors who had asked her to write to them. She became a devoted friend of sailors, forming the Royal Sailors' Rests. She published a monthly magazine, *Ashore and Afloat*, and established temperance societies on naval ships by personally making visits to ships when at the time; every ship had a grog pot. Aggie Weston was held in high esteem by all those who served in the Royal Navy and still draws the same respect today.

On the last Monday of July 1970, I began my specialist training. The division was reduced dramatically as others were going into different careers within the Navy and they were moved to their respective training bases. Specialist training for marine engineers took place at HMS Raleigh and was very much classroom based but had the added attraction of using simulators and a decommissioned warship to give us recruits a real taste of our future careers and of the environments in which we would be working and possibly fighting from. The latest technology was used to make classroom learning interesting and interactive. For the next six weeks, we continued to develop literacy and numeracy skills as well as learning about engineering. We covered steam, gas, diesel, and nuclear propulsion, how energy was transferred to drive the engines and other auxiliary equipment necessary to keep a warship going and how to tackle breakdowns when at sea or when in action.

You have to imagine a ship is like a small town or city, having to be totally self-contained, apart from food and fuel. Marine engineering was not just about enabling a ship to move in water but also about providing electricity, water, the ability to cook, dispose of waste products and providing power to other equipment like catapults on fixed winged carriers. We had to understand how to maintain sea water pressure for the hydrant systems used to fight any potential fires and how to make parts to fix any damaged mechanical items. Although training was as practical and active as possible, it did prove to be physically and mentally challenging with a focus on teamwork as well as on individual development. It was not only enjoyable and rewarding, but there was also an underpinning sense of military discipline, integrity and personal pride.

One of the decommissioned cruisers was used for on board training and so we had some experience of working in a boiler room, within an engine room, on auxiliary machinery, and on ships boats etc. We also had further instruction on fire fighting and damage control.

The first active part of our training was to understand the boiler system and how the boiler serviced nearly all of the equipment essential on board a ship. We also learned how to respond to immediate changes in speed and direction. We were introduced to the Admiralty three drum boiler which was huge. Not only did we have to heat water to make steam under pressure, the steam then had to be super-heated and further pressurised to drive the steam turbine engines. Steam turbine engines required pressurised dry steam which then hit turbines driving the engine that drove the propellers. If wet pressurised steam hit the engine turbines, this would be catastrophic, potentially breaking off turbine blades and destroying the engine. We worked on steam generators which provided electrical power, low pressure boilers to heat water for the galley, laundry and showers; cold water pumps used to feed the firefighting system and for hoses used on top deck for general purposes. We were introduced to evaporation systems which provided fresh drinking water, converting sea water to the purest water I have ever tasted. We learned of refrigeration systems, air conditioning systems and extraction units that removed toxic air. The bilge system cleared unwanted water from the ship and portable bilge pumps which were used in times of emergency to help stop a ship from sinking.

It is interesting how New Recruits and those just starting their basic training looked upon us, specialist training recruits as seasoned sailors, when the truth was; we were only twelve weeks in advance of them. Maybe it's because we were slicker in our marching or that we had somehow matured above those who were still undergoing basic training.

By the end of specialist training we were seen as being competent enough to join one of Her Majesty's war ships. We had to prepare for a second Passing Out Parade and another move from specialist training barracks to the ship's ratings division where we were ready for our first real deployment.

Our second passing out parade was similar to the first, but this time, there were less of us presenting as guard of honour and many newer recruits watching on. Of course, my mother and sister-in-law came to see me and the event went extremely well. The difference this time was that I was able to take time off after the parade to spend time with my family in Plymouth. For two days, I was able to stroll with my family around Plymouth Sound and relax before starting the next stage of my journey.

Chapter Three
A Naval Rating and Deployment

From mid-August until October, we remained at HMS Raleigh where we became 'Ships Company'. We were allocated different jobs on a daily basis. Sometimes carrying out guard duties at the main gate, other times cleaning roads, fixing broken equipment, babysitting New Entrants or just being general dog's bodies. In September, we were given more shore leave and a warrant to travel home. We still had to keep wearing uniform whilst at home but were told that once deployed to our next ship, we could wear civilian clothes whilst on leave in the UK. During this leave, CPO Giddings called to visit my mother along with his wife and children. I felt quite honoured to have my old divisional chief come visit and my family appeared to be the same. Little did I know that this would be the last time I saw Chief Giddings for quite some time.

On returning to Raleigh, we were told that we should be preparing for deployment and that very soon we would be moving to join our new ships. Part of the preparation was to get vaccinations and passports. We were informed that we had to collect our passports when we received our next wages. Payday was always a good day, even though wages had increased slightly, it really wasn't sufficient to buy all that we needed. One positive was that we were allowed a tobacco ration, 300 Blue Liners (tipped or plain), or five large tins of hand rolling tobacco or pipe tobacco. Most of us chose to have 200 Blue Liners and a small tin of hand rolling tobacco for when the 'tailor made' (normal cigarettes) ran out. We were also sent for our inoculations. Having to be inoculated to travel abroad in those days was not a pleasant experience. We collected our passports as instructed when we collected our pay and then were called to the sickbay where we mustered in an adjoining Nissan hut. There we were told to strip naked and when ordered, were to step through a door into another Nissan hut with hands on our hips. As each rating went through the door, we were injected in both arms and both legs and two more in the backside for good measure by strategically stationed naval nurses, then ordered to march one step forward to have a sugar lump forced into our mouths before having our medical record marked and signed off. We then exited to an outside door and marched back to our point of entry where we were ordered to dress. Marching outside stark naked was never my idea of fun as there was always numerous other ratings somewhere about marching and getting an eyeful.

During the last week of October 1970, 'we got our orders'. I, along with eight others had been ordered to join HMS Albion, (R07), and nicknamed 'The Old Grey Ghost of the Borneo Coast'. HMS Albion was a 22,000-ton centaur-class light fleet carrier of the Royal Navy. Originally, *Albion* was a fixed-wing carrier with a complement of 806 squadron comprising eight Sea Hawk FGA6 Fighter-Attack planes, 894 squadron comprising 12 Sea Venom FAW21 Night/All Weather Fighters, 849 squadron; D flight, four Sky raider AEW1 Airborne Early Warning aircraft, 815 squadron, with eight Whirlwind HAS7 Helicopter Anti-Submarine Warfare and Ships Flight 1 Dragonfly HR5 Helicopter Search and Rescue. In January 1961, conversion begun for the Albion to become a commando carrier and she was re-commissioned in 1962 and was joined by 40 Commando Royal Marines and all of their equipment with 848 and 846 helicopter squadrons. From henceforth, HMS Albion was known as a commando carrier. We had been told that for those of us joining HMS Albion, it was likely that we would not be seeing UK shores for some considerable time. I remember writing to my mother explaining where I was being deployed and the fact that I might not be returning for a while. The following weekend, my mother, along with my sister-in-law came to say farewell and wish me bon voyage. It was evident that my mother found this time extremely distressing, but for me it was exactly what I wanted to do. The following week we were told that we were being transported to Brize Norton where we would stay overnight and fly the next morning to Malta to meet our ship.

On the day of departure from HMS Raleigh we boarded a Royal Naval Coach and drove to RAF Brize Norton. RAF Brize Norton is located in Oxfordshire, about 75 miles west north-west of London. I remember the drive being long and noisy as all on board (except the driver) were eagerly anticipating their first ever flight. We arrived at our barracks at RAF Brize Norton during the early evening and were shown to our bunks before having dinner. After dinner, we were allowed to wander but told not to leave the base. I, along with Tansy Lee and

Tim Whitehouse decided to walk the airfield perimeter fence. It was a dry, albeit cold night but we had much fun as we walked along. About halfway, around the runway perimeter and just past the hanger bays, we found an unlocked gate. The gate was open and so we decided to go through the gate to take a better look at what was going on, natural curiosity always driving us forward and wanting to see what was ahead in the darkness. Because of the darkness, we headed towards lights in the far distance. We walked for quite a while before coming across huge hangers where a number of aircraft was stored. On entering the first hanger, we stood in awe of the aircraft on display. Having spent about half an hour looking at these marvellous machines, we exited the hanger into a second hanger and then a third then on to the runway located at the end of the third hanger. There, to our amazement, were a number of transporter planes being loaded with military equipment and other military transport and machinery. Watching what was going on for a while, we then saw this light grey mini cooper with the RAF target logo on its bonnet and roof, come bombing along at considerable speed towards us. The mini abruptly stopped just a few feet from where we stood and out jumped an Air Commodore. We immediately stood to attention and saluted, as is the nature of ratings when seeing a commissioned officer.

"What the fuck and how the fuck did you get here?" boomed the Air Commodore.

"We just came to have a look what was going on," we replied in unison.

"Well how did you get here?" the Commodore asked.

"Well," we said, "we were taking a stroll and as we walked along the perimeter fence, we saw this open gate and just walked through the gate in the fence," we replied.

"You did what?" he shouted. "And how long have you been here?" the Commodore asked.

"We've only been here about half an hour," was our response, "but we were in the hangers for about an hour before getting here," we said.

"Never mind," shouted the Commodore in an angry tone. "Stay there and shut up," the Commodore ordered.

The next thing we knew, the Commodore had called security and with that, Air Police cars came rushing towards where we were standing. We were then arrested and bundled into the awaiting police cars. We were driven to a large administration building, made to wait for about an hour and taken to the Commodores' office. We had to explain to the Commodore why we were in

Brize Norton and gave a full rundown of all of our movements since arriving at the base and where our ultimate destination was to be.

After the grilling from the Air Commodore, we were escorted back to our barracks under armed guard where we collected our draft papers and then returned back to the Air Commodore's office where we had to present them to the Air Commodore. The Air Commodore was fuming. Apparently (we found out later), the loading of the transporters had supposed to have been a very highly secretive operation and the areas we had accessed were totally out of bounds. We also found out that numerous extra guards had been put on patrol to prevent any onlookers from gaining access.

As we had not seen any guards during our foray and because the gate we went through was already open, we hadn't seen any problem in what we had done. After a few hours, we were allowed back to our barracks to rest before catching our flight the next day. Needless to say, the Air Commodore ensured that we were guarded up to the point of boarding our aircraft.

The flight aboard a brand new DC 10 was awesome. In many ways, the flight from Brize Norton was similar to that travelling on a civilian airliner. We had allocated seats, had instruction on safety measures and were well looked after by air stewards. We were served soft drinks during our flight and we also had a meal. To me, this is how I had envisaged royalty travelling and felt so special. The take-off was exhilarating and as I had been allocated a window seat, my head was permanently wedged in the window. I didn't want to miss anything. The flight was uneventful really, but flying for the first time I was spellbound by the cloud formation and of the views I saw flying over Europe. I recall the landing so vividly, because as we flew towards Malta, we actually flew over the island. We were descending then turned sharply over the Mediterranean Sea towards our landing point. The sea looked so amazingly blue, a deep sapphire blue, bluer than I had ever seen. This was a far cry from the brown waters of the English Channel and of the Atlantic Ocean. As we approached the runway, it seemed as if we were going to fly into the Clift edge, hurtling at speed to our impending death, but we landed safely on top and touchdown was fast and steady.

When we disembarked the aircraft, we were then taken to the main airport building where we presented our passports to immigration, had our passports stamped then collected by coach to travel to Valetta Harbour where HMS Albion was tied up alongside. As we drove into the harbour, our first sight was of St

Angelo, standing proud at the far side of the harbour. Fort St Angelo is a bastioned fort in Birgu, Malta. It is located at the centre of the Grand Harbour and was originally built in the medieval period as a castle called the Castrum Maris. HMS Albion sat at the opposite end of the Grand Harbour. When Albion came into view, my excitement was overwhelming and beyond belief. As our coach pulled up alongside the ship, the sight, size and enormity of this vessel began to sink in. This huge ship was to be my home and I was so happy to become part of the ship's company and of the ship's history. This ship was to take me to places far beyond what I had imagined and it was a place where many happy memories would be nurtured.

We collected our kit from the rear of the coach and marched up the gangway onto the ship. This was even more exciting than the flight to Malta. The name HMS Albion was strewn up on each side of the gangways [there were two (one foreword and one aft)]. On boarding, we saluted (as is custom when going on board) then saluted again to the Officer of the Watch. We presented our papers to the officer on watch who then checked us off on his itinerary; we were then led by one of the duty ratings to the main hanger.

In the hanger numerous helicopters, Wessex fives, Sioux, Wasps and Sea Kings were lined up and stored. Their rota blades folded back and covered and all securely strapped to the deck of the hanger. I was able to identify each of the helicopters from pictures that I had seen during training and actually seeing some of these helicopters when they landed at HMS Raleigh. In the hanger, two huge lifts were located; these lifts took the helicopters and other equipment from the hanger to the flight deck. The far lift was up and level with the flight deck, the bottom lift down and level with the hanger deck. I remember just how warm it was and of the warm breeze which was coming down the lift shaft. At the bottom of the lift which was down, sat at desks was an officer, the Jossman (Master at Arms, equivalent to a Police Chief Inspector in Civvie Street) and two scribes (ratings that were office based but worked on the ship). We were ordered to move forward but before we had time to join the queue to register, the Joss' shouted my name, Tim's Name and Tansy's name.

"Here sir," we shouted back.

He called us to one side, told us to leave our gear where it was, then marched us off the hanger deck along the main corridor of the ship until we reached the fore of the ship. There we were told to stop and wait outside of one of the doors. On the door was a highly polished wooded sign saying 'Captain's Office'. The three of us stood outside the door waiting and looking at each other with some nervousness. The Joss knocked on the door, entered and then closed the door. The next thing, the door opened and we were marched into the Captain's Office. We were called to a halt and stood in front of a large desk. Stood behind the desk was the Captain and two more officers.

"Salute!" ordered the Joss.

Like clockwork the three of us saluted in unison. We had no idea why were had been called to see the Captain, perhaps we were the youngest to join his ship and therefore had been given preferential treatment.

"So," said the Captain, "you're the three idiots who have broken the Official Secrets Act!" We all looked in shock. "You have trespassed into areas that were strictly forbidden and had the audacity to stand and watch proceedings on one of Her Majesty's RAF bases while very sensitive operations were underway, what do you have to say for yourselves?"

Nervously, we recalled the events of the previous evening, each adding in bits and pieces of the events as they had unfolded. At the end of our reiteration, there was a short silence. The Captain looked at the Joss (who had a slight smirk on his face) then looked at the three of us who were literally 'shitting ourselves'. "Well," the Captain said, "I have had a very irate Air Commodore from RAF Brize Norton on the phone to me and he was furious."

The Captain looked at the three of us in the eye and asked, "Did you not see any of the signs telling you that the area was strictly out of bounds? Or did you not see any of the guards?" the Captain asked.

"There were no signs or guards, sir," we replied in unison.

"Well," said the Captain, "I will take your word for it this time, but let me assure you, if any of you step out of line with me, your heads will be on the chopping block. I know from the Air Commodore that heads will be rolling in Oxford and by luck, you will be keeping yours. Welcome aboard, dismissed."

The Joss ordered us to about turn and we were marched out of the Captain's office. The Joss then took us back to the hanger to register.

On the way back to the hanger, the Joss smiled at us and said, "Bloody good job guys, those Brylcreem boys ain't got a clue, the Navy will always be the senior service, you've definitely put the cat amongst the pigeons."

Tim, Tansy and I looked at each other and smiled but were visibly shaken by the encounter with the Captain and at the quickness in which the Air Commodore had contacted our Captain. The Joss informed us not to worry and that the encounter with the Captain had just been a formality. He told us that the Captain had to be seen to have responded to the Air Commodore's request and that the Captain had already got all of the facts about our previous night's activities. Apparently, the Joss told us, there had been a double guard on duty that night and there had also been dogs on patrol. All of which had not seen the three of us moseying about around top secret operations. When we finally returned to the hanger, our orders were taken and we were allocated our mess. Ratings from various messes were on hand to take us to out allocated bunks. LMEM (Leading Hand Marine Engineering Mechanic, equivalent to a corporal in the Army) Beard was my mess leader and was there to point me in the right direction. LMEM Beard was an old guy who had been in the Navy for over 20 years and who was due to retire on our return to the UK. The years had not been kind to 'Beardy' as he was known, who in his 40s looked as if he was his 60s. Beardy took me to mess 23, towards the stern of the ship. The mess was located on a lower deck and housed 24 ratings. There was one empty bunk which was the lower of three.

"Here's your bunk," said Beardy. "I'll take you to the locker room and show you where your locker is. You can then unpack, get into your eights and I will take you to the galley to get some scran. Don't forget to bring your towel and wash gear, you will need it. By the way 'skin' (a term used in the Navy for young ratings who didn't require a shave), what's your name?"

"Graham," I replied.

"Well, from now on, you'll be called 'young Brummie'."

As I don't come from Birmingham I couldn't understand this, but accepted as if it was a natural progression. I suppose having a Black Country Accent is similar to the Birmingham accent but I recognised that others maybe wouldn't know where the Black Country was geographically or in relation to its proximity to Birmingham.

When I had unpacked, Beardy took me to the shower area and showed me were the heads were (toilets are known as heads in the navy), I then changed into my eights and returned back to the mess. Most of the occupants of the mess were on a 'run ashore' (gone out for the evening), others were on duty. Only one other rating was in the mess when I returned, 'Scotty' a guy from Glasgow.

He welcomed me to the mess and said, "The guys are going to love you." He laughed and Beardy also laughed along with him.

Beardy said, "Come on then, let's get you fed."

"Sees you later," Scotty said and I nodded.

In the Galley, I met up with Tim and Tansy. We chatted about our different messes, what the guys were like and of what had happened to each of us when we parted company at the hanger deck. We were all so excited and so happy to be on our first ship. We ate a dinner of steak and chips and had a pudding of chocolate sponge and custard. After a little while, we decided to go back to our respective messes to 'turn in' (going to bed). It had been a long and exhausting day and we all needed sleep. Once in my bed (pit), Beardy came over and we chatted for a while. He told me that there was a possibility that I would be moving to a new mess in a couple of days and that all new junior ratings would be put together. He also told me that he, along with some of the other ratings would be taking me on a run ashore the next night and would be introducing me the sights, smells and attractions of Malta. By the time the guys from the mess had returned from their run ashore or had come off duty, I was fast asleep.

The next morning, I was woken at 6:30 am to get ready for my first day of duty. The guys who had been on duty the previous night and some of those who had been ashore greeted me asking lots of questions about who I was, where I was from and about my journey to meet the ship. They all laughed when I recalled the happenings at RAF Brize Norton and about our greeting by the Captain.

"Trust the Navy to get one over the RAF," one guy said, then many more made various derogatory comments about the RAF.

"You coming ashore tonight?" I was asked.

"I don't know," I replied.

I hadn't got a clue about what I was or was not allowed to do.

"You'll find out today whether you are being given shore leave and if you do get it, we'll make sure that you're OK. You won't go wrong with us, we'll look after you."

Beardy told me that after breakfast, he would be taking me to the Machine Shop where I would be told what was expected of the new 'Stokers'. 'Stokers' was the name given to all Marine Engineering Mechanics in the Navy, a name passed down from when ships were coal driven and when most of the shovelling was done by our trade.

At breakfast, I met up with all the guys who had joined the ship the previous day; Cooks, Stewards, Electricians, Seamen and Stokers. We all intermingled until we were called to order and separated. Us Stokers were taken to the

Machine Shop where a rather stern looking Chief Petty Officer awaited us. We were told that for the next few days, we would be given a full guided tour of the ship and that we were to memorise all of the information given to us. After we had become familiarised and acquainted with the ship, we would then be given our place of work. We were also told that we would start at 0800 whilst getting used to the ship and then after would be given a rota of our watches. We were led off in groups of four and guided by one of the Killicks (Leading Hands). Our group started foreword of the ship and progressed towards the stern. We started in the 'Tiller Flat', a place where the anchors were stored when at sea. Here we were told that the anchors are discharged by gravity but hauled back into their storage by winch, which was steam driven. Steam from the boiler room was fed through the ship through a large pipe system. This steam also fed the galley kitchen and laundry. Other large pipes contained sea water, pressurised for the fire system and to be used in the 'Heads' (Toilets) for flushing. We visited the Galley kitchen and saw how steam was used for cooking, the laundry and the 'Ice Room'. Ice was made in vast quantities and stored in blocks. The ice was used in the Galley kitchen but was also available to the ships company. As a junior rating, it would be our job to collect ice for the mess. Ice was used to keep the beer cold as there was no room for fridges. We were taken to the generator rooms, there were several on board, each able to produce enough electricity to feed a small town. Information about how these diesel generators worked was given and what our role would be in maintaining electricity for the ship in conjunction with the 'Leckies' (Electricians). We visited the Arms bays, where a variety of missiles were kept, then on to the engine room. In the Engine room, we were introduced to the heart of the ship. The engines of which there were two were huge. Pipe work led to and from each engine all of which were clad in asbestos and painted brilliant white. The place was immaculately clean. Brass gauges were highly polished and the floors scrubbed to perfection. Officers in white overalls directed stokers in blue overalls to carry out a variety of tasks. Also in the engine room was evaporators. These evaporators converted sea water to fresh water for use throughout the ship. Given that there was a compliment of approximately 1596 crew on board when the air groups and Marines were on board, the use of fresh water was colossal. After visiting the Engine Rooms, we broke for lunch. During lunch, the new crew ate and exchanged the things that they remembered. There was so much to soak in. After lunch, we visited the Boiler Rooms. There were four boilers situated in two boiler rooms. We had to climb down to the boiler rooms after individually going through an air lock. The airlock was entered through a thick steel door that had to be closed tightly before opening another door to enter the boiler room. This second door had to be firmly closed before the next person could gain access. The Admiralty three drum boilers were also huge, set up in a triangular configuration. The two lower boilers produced steam from water and as the steam rose into the top boiler, this was further heated under pressure to produce dry steam that drove the engines. We were informed that when at sea, there was always a duty Petty Officer in charge and two stokers to control the burn for the boilers. After spending over an hour in the boiler room we were taken into the bowels of the ship, five decks down from the main runway, to see the prop shaft and the gears that supported the prop which then turned the propellers. I still recall how awe-inspiring this day had been but had not fully considered what it would actually be like when at sea and at full-steam ahead. After visiting the hangers and flight deck, we returned to the machine shop where we were presented with our very own 'monkey spanners'. Monkey spanners were the stoker's identification tool. Monkey spanners were actually wheel spanners, enabling the opening and closing of valves around the ship. There were a variety of different sizes of monkey spanners available in different areas of the ship, but for personal use, the 12" spanner could easily be carried and fitted the majority of valves that strewn the ship. Getting this spanner was like winning Olympic gold. It became a third hand and was treasured by each marine engineer. We were then told that the rest of the evening was ours and that we could take shore leave. We were told that we must carry our ID cards from now on and that if going ashore, we would need our IDs to enter the Dock Yard and to be allowed back on board ship.

After dinner, a group from the mess took me ashore. The first port of call was a small bar in Valetta Harbour. One or two of the guys had not eaten and ordered some food. One of the guys ordered fried eggs. When it arrived, there were 12 eggs fried on a plate, this was the first time that I had seen anyone eat so many eggs in one go. Apparently, this guy ate eggs before he went out drinking and to cure hangovers. We laughed as he devoured his eggs and the rest of us had beers. It felt so good being with a group of people who were like minded and who shared similar senses of humour. Someone suggested that later we had a trip down the 'Gut'. Fascinated by this, I ask what the 'Gut' was.

"Oh, you'll love the 'Gut', it's a street of bars and places to eat and have a good time."

Everyone who had been to the 'Gut' laughed. For those of us who had never been or had never heard of the 'Gut', we were at a loss of the joke. As it happened, we stayed in the bar all evening drinking. Towards the end of the night, people drifted off to various places or returned to the ship. The newest ship's company elected to go back to the ship with the proviso that we could be taken to the 'Gut' on another occasion. The short walk back to the ship was relaxing. The warmth of the Mediterranean sun during the day had left warmth radiating from the walls of the surrounding buildings and a warm gentle breeze blew around the Grand Harbour. How different Malta was to good old Blighty. At home it was cold, wet and miserable; here it was warm, dry and tranquil.

The next few days were spent on board ship and were devoted to learning more about the ship, as well as being tested on the knowledge we had gained. I didn't go ashore the following evening as funds were low and I decided to write home. Writing a letter home became a regular occurrence and for many, writing in the galley mess after meals had been completed was almost a social occasion. When writing home, we often shared our escapades so that we could spin our own perspectives on these events when writing and also share our feelings, which was so therapeutic. Some guys were homesick and feeling a little depressed, others elated and feeling overjoyed but what was interesting, whatever someone was feeling, others would always be there to share and support. At the weekend, we were given more time off. We had the whole weekend, Friday night, Saturday and Sunday to explore. We were reminded that although we did not have to report for duty on Sunday, we needed to be wide awake and fresh for Monday morning, so drinking on Sunday had to be limited.

On Friday night, I was taken ashore with members of my mess and this time we were heading for the main town. After a few drinks in the bars by the harbour, we moved into the centre of town. Malta is a beautiful place with buildings on antiquity. There was a relaxed feeling everywhere one went and it was easy to understand the currency then as Malta was using Imperial Great British pounds, shillings and pence. After wandering around and stopping occasionally for beer, we were then led to a very narrow street, so narrow that it was difficult for two people to walk abreast. The cobbled street had bars all the way down on either side and we were taken into a number of these as the night went on. Older ratings were greeted by name from the bar owners and their waiters and the newbies were introduced to the bar staff by these older crew members. About half way down the Gut, there was a building on the right hand side, with a green door. "Come on lads, let's take the skins in for some fun," someone shouted.

The older guys laughed and hurried us, the newbies, inside. Just inside the door sat an elderly woman. The woman, who was dressed in all black, greeted the older guys as if she had known them all personally for years.

"What are you having boys?" said the woman.

"We're treating our new ship mates. They have never been here and we want to teach them the ropes," a reply came from one of the guys.

The woman eyed us newbies and smiled. Some money then exchanged hands between the older guys and the woman.

"Rooms six, seven and eight; and no rough stuff," the woman said.

I was pushed up a flight of stairs to where room six was situated. The guys with me knocked the door and pushed me inside. It was at this stage that it dawned on me that this was a brothel. Being naive to these sorts of things, I hadn't a clue what to do.

"Enjoy son, we'll meet you downstairs," and the door was closed behind me.

In the dim light I saw a woman lying half naked.

"Come in sweetie, you're very young."

"Yes, I replied, I'm only 16."

"Well I'm Lolita," said the woman.

"Hello," I replied nervously. "I'm Graham, but my mates call me Brummie."

"That's nice," Lolita replied. "I know a lot of Brummie's. What would you like to do sweetie?" the woman asked.

"I'm not sure," I replied.

Having never been in a situation like this before and being extremely nervous I said, "Do you like playing cards?"

The half-clad woman laughed and said, "Yes, I do."

To my amazement Lolita pulled a pack of playing cards from a drawn set in a bedside table.

"What shall we play?" asked Lolita. "How's about we play strip polka?" Lolita said with a laugh.

"Ummm, I'd rather play Rummy if you don't mind!" I stated very quickly and rather embarrassingly.

"OK baby, whatever you say," Lolita responded.

We began playing and agreed stakes of no more than a shilling. As we played, I was reminded of the many rimes I had played cards at home with my mother, but this had a very different feel about it. We played cards for about 45 minutes, making small bets on each hand. After the time allocated, I was told that I had to leave as my time was up. Lolita, smiled and thanked me, gave me a gentle kiss on my cheek while at the same time squeezed my bum. My face must have turned crimson but I was happy to leave because I felt that I had met a really good friend and had also benefitted from my visit by winning ten shillings for the pleasure of being there.

Lolita kissed me one more time on my forehead and said, "I hope to see you again soon."

I left the room smiling but had totally forgotten about the other guys who said that they would be waiting for me downstairs.

When I eventually reached the bottom of the stairs, the guys began cheering and patting me on my back saying, "Well done, son."

I didn't have the nerve to tell them what had really happened, but I did say that I had had a really great time and that I had been invited back. We left the 'Green Door' and after having a few more drinks, returned to the ship. I never returned to the 'Green Door' but the memory of that night remains fixed in my memory. I also never told anyone else about what had happened in Lolita's room or about my winnings. Some secrets are best as secrets, which is what I say.

After a few more days in Malta harbour and working from the machine shop, I was then assigned my new full-time duties as an Auxiliary Stoker. My job after two days' training was to visit each and every compartment where there was mechanical machinery and to take readings from all of the gauges. The job meant that I had to walk for miles, climbing up and down ladders, from foreword to stern, recoding accurately and reporting any deviations in the readings to the duty Engineering Officer. Each set of 'rounds' took two hours and I was rotor'd to work watches. I began my watches doing 'Dogs, Middle and Forenoon' then 24 hours off. Then 'Afternoon, First and Morning' followed by another day off. This rotor was to be my constant programme of work for quite some considerable time and my role would continue at sea and when we were in harbour. The 'Dog' watches begin at 1600 hours. The first 'Dog' watch lasted until 1800 and the second 'Dog' watch from 1800 hours until 2000 hours. This was followed by the 'First watch, 2000 hours until midnight, the 'Middle' watch from midnight until 0001 hours (There is no 0000 midnight in the navy), and the 'Morning' watch from 0400 hours until 0800 hours, the 'Forenoon' from 0800 hours until midday and the 'Afternoon' from midday until 1600 hours. This way of working was difficult to get used to, as there was little time to sleep. After each watch was completed, we had just enough time to shower, wash underwear and socks, get food or just turn in ('turning in' getting some sleep).

When we slept, we were always woken by our 'opposite number' (the other guy working the opposite watches) 30 minutes before we were due to commence work. This gave just enough time to take a quick wash, dress and grab a drink before commencing our next watch. Being the Auxiliary Stoker held with it lots of responsibility. It was a lonely existence and at times quite creepy, especially when having to take reading in places like the prop shaft, which was five decks below the water line and was always noisy and cold. Being all alone at night on a noisy ship played havoc on one's psyche. I was always looking around expecting something untoward to happen or for someone to jump out when I least expected it. There were benefits too, in that you would meet with lots of other people on your travels that you might never see if based in just one area like the engine room or boiler room. After a short period of time, I was well known by all of the Marine Engineering Department and many of the other ratings from different departments.

The day before we left Malta, I was moved from the mess I had been allocated and joined a new mess allocated for junior ratings. This was great, as all of the guys in this mess were of, or about the same age as me. The only person who was older was the 'Mess Killick', Johno, who was quite a miserable guy and who rarely ever spoke. The only time he verbalised anything was in giving orders to clean up or to go collect things for the mess.

We set sail from Malta and headed for Greece, my first real voyage at sea on a warship, what a buzz. The noise of the engines produced a loud humming sound which reverberated throughout the ship. There was even a sensation of movement forward, even though the sea was calm and peaceful. Being at sea for the first time was a greater pleasure than I could have imagined and being at sea in the Mediterranean was a great pre-curser to things that were to come.

We were heading for Athens to pay an official visit. Official visits were nearly always short lived but this did restrict the opportunities for runs ashore. My shore leave in Athens was short but enabled me to visit the Parthenon. In the 1970s you were able to walk and stroll around the Acropolis and Parthenon. Restoration on these magnificent buildings had not begun at this time and I feel privileged to have been able to visit these incredible monuments before restrictions were put in place. Athens was a busy city and I was able to purchase a few mementos for my mother. The heat in Athens was quite oppressive. There appeared to be so much traffic around Athens giving off fumes which created a fog like atmosphere and which increased the temperature in the city. I was glad that it was not the height of summer as I do not think that it would have been such a pleasant time to visit this great city. The people of Athens were very welcoming of the British navy and many people wanted to say hello and to show their generous hospitality. We drank Mythos beer to keep us cool and the food was just excellent. My first visit to Greece made me a lifelong fan of this country and of its people.

As we left Athens, I recall finding a place on one of the upper decks to watch as the city faded in the distance. We were sailing to Cyprus for planned exercises. These exercises took place at sea with other NATO forces. This was the first time I had been involved with such activities and the workload on board increased dramatically. Not only was I carrying out my duties as an auxiliary stoker, I was also called up to act as a firefighter and damage control worker in simulated exercises. There were simulated attacks which provided the ships company to respond; sometimes this meant that we had to pretend that the ship had been struck by missiles from other ships and aircraft. Our response to these simulations was critical. This also meant that rest time was limited and our alertness increased. The Royal Marines also carried out joint exercises on land. The flight deck was constantly busy with helicopters flying on and off the ship almost nonstop, both day and night. Extra pressure was put on the marine engineers' department to maintain functioning of all systems particularly on the flight deck.

After the completion of the exercises, the ship anchored off Limassol. As the ship was far too large to pull alongside any of the docks, we had to take liberty boats to have a run ashore. These liberty boats ferried us to the coast, dropping us off at local jetties. Limassol lies on Akrotiri Bay (the British have a large RAF base at Akritiri), on the southern coast, southwest of Nicosia; it is the island's second largest city. Although being the second city in Cyprus, there was not much activity going on at that time in Limassol. At the start of the 1970s, Limassol was becoming a new home to many thousands of prosperous Arab refugees from Lebanon and immigrants from Saudi Arabia and Kuwait. Limassol had a bustling port with many distribution warehouses. Limassol was becoming known for its exports in wines, beverages, fruits, and vegetables. Legumes, vegetables, oranges, lemons, grapefruits, nuts, and apples which were grown locally were everywhere to be seen. Bricks, tiles, shoes, textiles, furniture, cement, buttons, and soft drinks were manufactured in Limassol and fruit is canned there. Chrome and asbestos are processed in Limassol. Because the nightlife was limited in Limassol, many of us grabbed taxis to Nicosia and Larnaca. This was before the Island was invaded by the Turks and the island was split. My preference was to visit Nicosia. Nicosia was some distance from Limassol and as a result, my visit to Nicosia was over two days. Down the side streets of Nicosia, many of the buildings looked as if they were crumbling, half-ruined or abandoned. Of course, not all of Nicosia is like this, but many places were pretty rundown. Although saddened by the sights of these buildings, I did spend a very productive day in Nicosia wandering around; enjoying the typical laidback Greek lifestyle and enjoying the Greek food. Later that evening, I joined a group of Royal Marines in one of the Tavernas where we enjoyed more food before beginning a night of drinking. As it happens, I wasn't the greatest drinker at the best of times and could not keep up with the pace of others within the group. And so, at about 10:00 pm, I took my leave of the group with the purpose of returning back to the ship. I must have had great difficulty walking or making any sense to the locals in trying to get transport back to the jetty. I was in a sorry state indeed and was at a loss on what I should do. Luckily, a kindly Marine found me wandering and took me under his wing (a term used within the Navy for someone being looked after). The Marine, was a bugler and someone I had met on board ship many times. He saw the state I was in and took me to a hotel so that I could sleep off the effects of the alcohol before returning to the ship. Bugler Saywell was to become a great friend and we would often go ashore together to visit the countries where we landed. The hotel was rather dilapidated, had plaster falling off the walls and there was a strong smell of damp. The beds in the hotel had seen better days and the mattresses tended to roll the sleeper into the middle. When we awoke the next morning, we laughed about the beds and how each had had difficulties getting out of his respective beds in order to go to the bathroom during the night. After having a breakfast, we further explored Nicosia before heading back to Limassol. It happens to many drunken sailors that someone will always look out for you and will make sure that you are safe and well, even if they have never met you before.

The weather had broken and we experienced torrential rain and gale force winds. When we arrived at Limassol, to where the liberty boats had been running, we found literally hundreds of Matelot's (Pronounced Matlot) which is another name for a naval rating), all gathered together. When we approached the group, we were told that there would not be any liberty boats because of adverse weather conditions and that the ship had had to up anchor and sail into deeper waters for safety reasons. We were told that we had to make our way to Famagusta, where, when the weather had settled, we would be able to re-join our ship. Famagusta is a considerable distance from Limassol but transport was laid on by the RAF which was based in Akrotiri. Akrotiri became the biggest base of its kind during the Cold War, defending NATO's southern flank. On arriving at Famagusta, we were off loaded near a jetty. The jetty appeared to be in the middle of nowhere, there were no buildings nearby and nowhere to shelter. The jetty was concrete built and had arches along its length to support the jetty road. All of us who ended up waiting at the jetty made homes for the night under the arches and built fires using drift wood to stay off the bighting wind. It was a great adventure and for someone of my age a real thrill. The next morning the weather changed and liberty boats began to arrive to transport us back to the ship. Even though we had spent the night 'roughing it', we were still expected to carry out our duties without any reprieve. Once everyone was accounted for, we sailed from Cyprus for Gibraltar. The trip to Gibraltar was a little rougher than the trip from Malta to Athens and from Athens to Cyprus but not unpleasant. I was looking forward to visiting Gibraltar and hoped for better weather when we arrived.

We docked in the centre of Gibraltar harbour. The ship arrived under procedure Alpha with the sun blazing. Procedure Alpha is where officers, commissioned and non-commissioned officers as well as ratings lined the edge of the flight deck in full dress uniform. As we docked, the Band of the Royal Marines played various marches, ending with the National Anthem. Ratings that were not on duty were expected to be available for this procedure and as we pulled alongside, crowds had gathered. The cheering from the crowds was awe-inspiring. Gibraltar's main street ran from the docks uphill to the top of the town. We could see people stopping in the street to see the arrival of the ship. We were only staying in Gibraltar for a matter of days for this official visit but Gibraltar's dignitary had been invited to attend a cocktail party on the evening of the second night. Luckily, I was allowed ashore on that night but saw many high profile politicians, naval personnel and officers from the RAF and Army arrive. As I went ashore, the band of the Royal Marines were playing as guests were provided with canapés and drinks. It sounded as if everyone was having a great time.

The older guys from previous mess were to be my guide for the night and as we headed up the hill, I was told that we were going to Jimmy's Bar. Apparently, Jimmy was infamous and his bar was a real favourite with all British sailors. When we arrived at Jimmy's, Jimmy was waiting at the door. Jimmy had long hair, perfectly groomed and dressed quite flamboyantly.

"Hi, Jimmy," shouted the guys.

"Hello boys," Jimmy responded, "I've been waiting for you all. I saw you arrive today and thought oh good, my boys are back."

Jimmy had a very feminine voice and was rather camp. As we got closer, you could see that Jimmy was wearing 'makeup'. This was the first time that I had ever seen a guy wearing makeup and to act in such an effeminate way.

"Hey Jimmy, we've brought you a present," shouted Jordie.

Jordie was one of my favourite characters in the mess. Hailing from Newcastle, he always had a smile on his face and was always cracking jokes. He was also a heavy drinker and often ended up fast asleep in the corner of some bar.

Jimmy said, "Jordie my love, you are a very naughty boy. You will frighten this poor child to death."

Everyone laughed but somehow the joke was lost on me. After being in the bar for only a short time, I could understand why this bar was a favourite with matelot's. The music was great, drinks were cheap and Jimmy would entertain everyone by impersonating various Hollywood movie stars, all female. Jimmy took time to come over to our table where I was introduced to him.

"Don't you worry about these guys, baby, I know them all and they are all very naughty boys. I'll make sure that you are safe and that they don't get you into trouble."

Again, laughter filled the room and through my embarrassment, I could see that there was a strong platonic friendship between all of the guys and Jimmy. Apparently, Jimmy had owned this bar for years and many of the older guys had known Jimmy almost as long as he had been there. Jimmy was famous for recognising his guests and could recall their names and dates when they had visited Gibraltar. He also remembered what ships the guys had been serving on at that time and of the friends they had been with. His memory was extraordinary. Jimmy sat with us for a while and related stories of each guy who had been in his bar previously. At the end of the night, Jimmy bade us goodnight throwing us out so that he could close. We carried Jordie back to the ship as he was sound asleep and had been for the final hour in Jimmy's bar.

The next day, I was able to visit 'The Rock'. The vista from the rock was stunning. You could see the whole of Gibraltar from the rock and the ship looked magnificent from the top of the rock. Barbary apes ran along the walls of the rock and stole food when they could. I was unable to return to Jimmy's bar that evening and I was on duty. Sadly, I never saw Jimmy again as we set sail the following day and I heard that not long after Jimmy had died. I am sure that Jimmy was mourned by countless matelot's when they heard the news of his death.

From Gibraltar, we set sail towards England. We stopped off at Brest in France for another official visit; I was keen to try out the little French I had learned at school. Sadly, the people of Brest were not very sociable or talkative. Wherever we went, the local people looked at us with scorn. I was not aware that during WWII Brest had been heavily bombed by the Allies and many civilians had been killed as well as almost flattening all of the buildings and houses in Brest, the memory of this was fixed firmly within the community's Psyche. We met up with some French sailors and had a drink with them, sharing the local wine (which tasted like vinegar) and had a few beers together. The French guys, like us were in uniform. I remember thinking how striking they all looked compared with us Brits. The French Navy uniform had style. Blue and white hooped tee shirts, and tight fitting jacket and trousers, which flared at the bottom and a white hat, trimmed around the edge in blue and a bright red pompom on the top of the hat held on with red tape giving a cross-like shape across the crown. Our uniform in comparison was rather scratchy and as it was winter dress, we were forced to wear our navy jumpers, which made you constantly itch as the jumpers were directly next to the skin.

The French you learn at school is not always the vocabulary you want when surrounded by French sailors, or trying to talk to the locals on the quayside in a seafaring port. If you want to brag about your adventures about crossing the Bay of Bisque or even crossing the English Channel in a force seven won't actually mean much, even to a French sailor. Equally trying to explain to a taxi driver in a French port that you need taking somewhere could create an international incident, especially if you sound a bit German and especially in Brest. Germans were hated even more than the British for obvious reasons. After all, it had only been 25 years since WWII had ended and many communities within France were still recovering and being re-built.

From Brest, we headed into Portsmouth. It took us around 12 hours to cross the English Channel to reach Portsmouth. I was looking forward to going to Portsmouth or 'Pompy' as it was known, for two reasons. Firstly, because I had never been to Portsmouth and had heard so much about this great naval city and the dockyard and secondly, I had heard so many stories on board about Pompy and its array of pubs and bars. Portsmouth was also home to HMS Victory, Admiral Lord Nelson's Flag ship, which was in dry dock in the centre of the dockyard. Our journey across the English Channel was rough and the ship rolled constantly from side to side as it moved ever forward. Even when we headed into Portsmouth, the sea continued to pound the ship. Winter at sea in rough conditions is something you had to get used to, or cope with perpetual seasickness.

We docked in Portsmouth Harbour in front of HMS Eagle. HMS Eagle was a fixed winged Aircraft Carrier and larger than the Albion. HMS Eagle and HMS Ark Royal were the two largest ships in Her Majesty's Navy at that time. The Albion and Bulwark the second largest. HMS Bulwark was the sister ship to HMS Albion and also a Centaur class vessel. It was mid-December and we were only in port for a few days. Even being in Portsmouth for a few days, I was still able to take some shore leave to explore Portsmouth and Southsea. The time in Portsmouth allowed me to get my bearings for when we returned to Portsmouth. We were preparing to sail north to join a large contingent of NATO ships in the Arctic. After just a few short few days, we left Portsmouth sailing up the Western coast of the UK, moving around Cornwall, up past Wales and Scotland's Western Islands then on towards the Shetlands before moving east and up following the coast of Norway, eventually arriving in the Barents Sea. The majority of Norway borders water, including the Skagerrak inlet to the south, the North Sea to the southwest, the North Atlantic Ocean (Norwegian Sea) to the west, and the Barents Sea to the north. The north eastern border of Norway meets Russia near the Norwegian coastal port of Kirkenes. We were in the Arctic during the Polar Night, during the polar night, there is no sunrise and the sun is below the horizon continuously for 24 hours or more. NATO had gathered in this area as a show of strength to the Russians, as the Cold War was still ongoing. On-board the Albion, one of the commando groups were housed and were being taken by helicopter towards Haarstad in Norway for Arctic war training.

As you can imagine, the temperature in the Arctic at that time of year was cold, but surprisingly not so cold as you imagine, however, when the dreaded polar lows sweep in suddenly and unexpectedly from the Arctic Ocean towards Norway it suddenly becomes cold, bloody cold. The sea was the roughest I had ever experienced. Swells of 40 feet were recorded and the ship rolled at such a pitch that as you walked along the 'main drag' (main thoroughfare), you would be walking on the deck, then on the bulkhead (wall), back to the deck and then along the opposite bulkhead. Several days of this was torture. As we ploughed through the swells, the noise from the engines changed constantly. This was because of the propellers having to work at different speeds dependent upon the position of the ship in relation to the swells. Working was near impossible, having to wait for each roll of the ship to waver before you could attempt to climb ladders, then to hold on as tight as possible as the ship rolled in the opposite direction before descending or ascending.

Operation 'Clockwork' turned out to be a huge success, albeit we were not aware of it at this stage. From the Arctic, we returned to the UK, stopping at Queens Ferry and HM Dockyard at Rosyth in Scotland. During the 1960s, Rosyth underwent a major defence re-alignment and became the designated major refitting base for the Polaris (strategic ballistic missile) nuclear submarine fleet, the dockyard being re-equipped to handle major servicing and refitting of the submarines and their reactors (but not the missiles and warheads). The base also remained important for the refitting and support of minor war vessels (mine countermeasures ships and patrol craft) while warships and auxiliaries of other types (and other NATO nations) visited the base for refit, resupply or in preparation for major exercises.

In Scotland; I, Timmy and Tansy met up with some of the local girls. The girl I was latched onto was a year older than me and at 17 years old; she already had two children, had been married and divorced. Whilst I found this meeting good fun, I didn't realise that my date was getting very emotionally involved with me. We had only met a few times and during those times had only hung around chatting. On our last day, she began crying, begging me to write to her and to come back to Scotland as soon as I could.

"Let's get married," she begged.

Shocked and surprised, I said, "I'll have to think on that one."

I have never been so pleased to leave a place in all my life and have never returned to Scotland since. From Rosyth we headed back to Portsmouth, this time travelling along the eastern coast of the UK. We were back in Portsmouth just a few days before Christmas and would be remaining here for about three months before heading out on our next tour of operations. In Portsmouth, some of the guys were given leave over the Christmas period, I remained on board as part of a 'skeleton crew'. My leave came after the return of the main body of the ships company. Christmas on board ship whilst in dock is very different to anything that I had experienced before during a holiday period. As there was only a skeleton crew, only the minimum number of crew were left and when not on duty, the number of crew reduced again by half. I remember there were very few people in the galley mess for Christmas dinner and only four of us in the mess during the evening, but we made the most of our evening eating chocolates and Christmas cake and drinking copious amounts of beer. Having worked Christmas, I was afforded the night off for New Year and celebrated 1971 in Guildhall Square. Sadly, through being too intoxicated, I cannot remember much about the celebrations apart from knowing that I had been there.

During early January I had several days at home. It was good to be home after the quiet Christmas and New Year aboard ship. I was able to recall my adventures to everyone I met, my trip to the Mediterranean, and to the Arctic Circle. I also had to prepare my family and inform them, that within weeks, I would be leaving the UK for the Far East. I had no idea how long I would be away, but was sure that it would be for about a year or even longer and of course I would not be seeing my home and family again for some considerable time.

Leaving home from my leave this time was quite strange. My mother and brothers all appeared happy and content about me going away, but there was an underlying feeling that they were concerned for me. After all, the cold war was still a threat and troubles around the world appeared to be escalating. I left home feeling refreshed and looking forward to sailing to hotter climes. In March 1971, HMS Albion was to set sail once again.

Chapter Four
Trouble Before We Left

HMS Albion, R07 was preparing to leave for the Far East and the whole ship's company were busy with preparations. The ship had to be fully sea-worthy, stocked up, re-painted and prepared for what was to lie ahead. We also welcomed a new Captain, Captain James Jungius RN. The immediate weeks before leaving Portsmouth, all of the ship's company took every opportunity to go ashore whenever possible, I was no exception. I, along with my opposite numbers, frequently stayed overnight at the Royal Sailors Rest, before returning back to the ship. There was something quite special about staying ashore during this time. It cost very little to stay overnight at the Sailors Rest where you were provided with a comfortable single bed in a very small cubicle. Each cubicle was separated by a thin wooded wall. For the first few hours you didn't get much rest because of the noise of people returning drunk from the local pubs. There were often loud chats, people shouting goodnight, some singing and then the falling of people as they struggled to undress before getting into their allotted beds. It seemed as if we were at sea again, mainly because when the men were getting undressed, they swayed, falling onto their beds and banging up against the thin walls. How those walls never collapsed, I will never know. Those who were totally inebriated must have slept with their clothes on because all you heard of them was the sound of their bodies hitting the bed and the springs clanking against the bed frames.

Three days before we set sail, I was on duty carrying out my tasks as required, going from forward to aft checking all or the gauges and taking measurements in each of the departments and recording my readings. I was on Afternoon, First and Morning. By 0800, I was exhausted and ready for some sleep. I had been in bed for just over an hour when I was woken up and told to report to the Jossman. I clambered into my eight's and made my way to the

Jossman's office. There I was met by the Jossman and two very large men dressed in civilian clothes. Also present was my Divisional Officer. I was marched into the Jossman's office where I was informed that I was being arrested on a charge of 'sabotage'. I was told not to say anything but was told that I had to accompany the two burly guys present to be interviewed by them. Apparently, they were civilian police inspectors from the Dockyard Police and as the ship was in dock, any policing was in their jurisdiction. My Divisional Officer said that he would be accompanying me to the Dockyard police station where he would represent me. To say that I was in shock was an understatement, *Me, sabotage? What the hell are they going on about?*

I was taken to the station booking in desk where I had to present my ID card. I was asked my name, number, rank and position on the ship. I was told that I was being held on suspicion of sabotage and dereliction of duty. I was told that at some time during the hours of 0400 and 0800 it was alleged that I had wilfully opened a valve to a lube oil tank and had flooded a machine shop with the intention of preventing HMS Albion from sailing. Or that I had neglected my duty by not checking the gauges to the lube oil tank at the appropriate time and as a result, had missed seeing that the lube oil tank had been tampered with and because of this, the machine shop had been flooded. I was confused and shaking. I was told that I would be interviewed and that anything that I said or refused to say could be used in evidence against me. I was then taken to a cell.

As a 16-year-old who had never been in any sort of trouble before, it felt that my world had totally collapsed. I was tired, frightened and emotional. Sitting in the cell, all I could do was to keep going through my mind every step and action I had taken during my watches and even when I was off duty. After an hour, the Divisional Officer came into the cell. He asked me if I was OK and then proceeded to tell me why I had been brought to the police station. The DO said that at around 0830, the machine shop CPO had gone into the machine shop and found that a valve to the lube oil tank had been opened fully and the contents of the tank had flooded the machine shop floor. As I was the only person to have had permission to go to the machine shop to carry out my role as Auxiliary stoker, it was assumed that I had opened the valve deliberately. The DO then said, if it was found that I had not tampered with the value, I had to explain how so much oil could have escaped from the lube oil tank given that I had to check this as part of rounds. I was immediately on the defensive, stating that I had not touched the valve in question and that I had carried out my role as required. I really had no idea how this could have happened. The DO said that the police officers would interview me but as my representative, the DO would be present throughout. The DO left the cell and my mind was quickly going over every minute of the morning watch. I recalled every step, trying to visualise the time I had gone to each compartment and of the readings of each gauge I had checked. In my mind's eye, I walked every step of the watch, even taking in time when I took a refreshment and toilet breaks. Another hour passed before the police officers called me to the interview room.

The interview was recorded. I had a sense of guilt hanging over me, although I was not guilty of doing anything wrong. The officers asked my name for the record, my ID number, my rank and position within the engineering department. The inspectors went through the alleged charges and then said, "OK, so we know that you did it. To save time for both you and us, admit that you did it and this will all be over and done with."

"But I didn't do anything," I replied.

"So, you didn't open the valve and you didn't check the machine shop as you were supposed to do?" one of the officers said.

"No I didn't open the valve and yes I did check everything that I was ordered to check," was my response.

"But you have just told us that you didn't do anything, which means that you either didn't open the valve or you didn't carry out your duties. Or was it that you did open the valve deliberately?" the inspector said.

"I did carry out my duties and I did not open the valve on the lube oil tank," I corrected myself quickly.

"Then if you didn't open the valve and you did carry out your duties to the letter, who did do it, who opened the valve?" the police officer retorted.

"I don't know," I said in frustration.

"Let's go through your watch," the officer said. "Minute by minute."

One thing that I was good at was recalling short term memory events, even though I was tired and upset. I gave my account of the four hour watch, even giving some of the readings I had taken and explaining how I could remember these readings with accuracy. When it came to taking readings from the lube oil tank in the machine room, I was able to give appropriate times when I entered the machine shop and measurements taken as well as an approximate time of leaving the machine shop. I stated that I had been to the machine shop twice during my duties, at approximately 0415 and again at approximately 0615 as required. I told them that I knew the precise reading in the lube tank as no lube oil had been used from the tank that day and all of the readings had been the same. I felt pleased with my concise response and felt that I had quantified my actions.

There was a slight pause, then the interviewing officer said, "If you did as you have stated, visited the machine room at 0615, how could so much oil escaped from the oil tank in the time that the valve was found to be open?"

How could I answer that question? I would have had to have been a genius to calculate the flow of oil from the tank and the time it would have taken for the amount of oil to have been released. As it happens, I didn't have a clue how much oil had gone from the tank, so I asked, "If you want me to try and work out the flow ratio of oil flow, you'll have to tell me the viscosity of the oil and the amount of oil found on the floor."

The DO laughed into his hand as the officers looked at each other.

"Now you're being fucking cocky. Just answer the question," the inspector shouted.

"I can't answer your question because I'm not a mathematical genius," I shouted back.

"It is our suspicion that you deliberately opened this value to prevent the ship from sailing because you did not want to spend a substantial amount of time away from the UK," the inspector said.

"That's rubbish," I argued.

I wanted more than anything to be travelling and I was actually looking forward to being in far off places. It had never come to mind that some people who had joined the navy would ever want to remain within the UK, it seemed totally illogical to me.

The inspectors began to go over the same line of questioning again and again. By late afternoon, I was at the point of breaking and would have said anything they asked. I was exhausted from having little sleep over the last 36 hours, had not eaten properly and was ready to burst into tears. *Not very promising* I thought if I was being interrogated by enemy captives. At this point, even the DO had had enough too. The DO put a stop to the questioning demanding that we all take a break. I was returned to my cell.

About an hour later, the DO came to my cell and said, "Come on, we are going back to the ship."

I asked if I had been released.

The DO said, "At the moment but you have not been fully cleared yet either. I don't think that there is sufficient evidence but we will have to wait to find out what will happen next."

We returned to the ship in silence. On-board, we went to the Joss's office where the DO related what had happened. You could see that the DO was not a happy man. I was told to go get some rest and also told not to worry about going back on my next set of watches as these had been covered. The DO remained with the Joss and I made my way back to the mess. After showering and getting some food, I crawled into my pit totally exhausted. I slept solidly for ten hours.

Not long after I woke up, I sat on my bed being questioned by my mess mates on what had happened to me. I told them in some detail of the events that had taken place and of my disbelief of what I had been accused of. I found it reassuring that at least my mess mates totally believed me and told me not to worry. There was the occasional joke being made relating to the episode, mainly about how many years I would have to spend in prison before being discharged and the fact that I should be grateful as in previous years, I would have been hung from the Yard Arm. Later that day, I received orders to go back to the Joss's office. There to greet me was the Joss, my DO, and the Chief of the machine shop as well as the First Lieutenant. To my relief, I was told that the investigation had progressed and that no further action was to be taken against me. The relief was overwhelming and I broke down.

The First Lieutenant said, "I have been told by your DO that you were excellent with your responses to the police and that you provided accurate evidence throughout."

He went on to apologise for the way I had been treated by the dock yard police as said that a report would be sent to their superiors with regard to my treatment. I asked if they had any idea how the oil had escaped but was told not to concern myself anymore with this matter. I was given the next two days off and told that I would resume my normal duties after my furlough. I returned to the mess and related to the guys what had happened in the Joss's office.

Scotty said, "You jammy bastard, two days furlough, I think I might go and flood the machine shop to see how many days off I can get."

We celebrated by having a beer. Things resumed back to normal, but I had been affected by the whole incident and from then on I became so cautious about what I did from then on. I never wanted a repartition of the last few days. To celebrate further, I went ashore that night. This was to be the last night in Portsmouth as the ship was due to sail the very next day.

Chapter Five
The Long Voyage

We set sail from Portsmouth in March 1971 for the Far East. Sailing out of Portsmouth under procedure Alpha we headed for the North Atlantic. We sailed close to the coast line of numerous countries but never close enough to see the coastline. We passed France, Northern Spain, Portugal, Morocco, the Canary Islands, Mauritania, Senegal, Gambia, Guinea Bissau and Sierra Leone before heading directly to Ascension. After several days, we had reached just north of the equator and sailed past St Helena.

Eventually, we reached the equator. Crossing the equator, or crossing the 'line' is a major event in the life of the Royal Navy. Naval tradition dictates that any ship crossing the equator must pay their respects to the Lord of the Seas, King Neptune to gain his acceptance. This ritual requires all those who had never crossed the equator (line) previously, to be charged for their crimes and get the justice they deserved. The ceremony starts on the previous night before the crossing with Davy Jones (usually, Davy Jones is played by an older none commissioned officer), the Bears (Davy Jones's trusted body guards) and the Police (not the real police) taking over the ship – all of which are actual senior ratings and who had previously crossed the line many times. Each mess on board is visited by Davy Jones and his entourage. All those who are 'charged' (those who had not previously crossed the line) are forced to stand, are physically held by the Bears or Police and the charges read out. You are then summoned to attend the ceremony the following day.

On the flight deck, preparations were also taking place for this prestigious event. In the centre of the flight deck, a canvas pool had been erected. The pool was approximately four-foot-deep and covered an area six foot by six foot. At one end of the pool stood a platform which had a dais, upon which two thrones had been placed. The thrones were highly decorated with gold plywood backing and strewed with paper and plastic seaweed. There was enough room to get about six people on the platform and fixed to the platform was a short plank of wood fitted with a small stool. The plank was strategically placed over the pool and the seat had been fixed to tilt backwards. Around the pool area were barriers and a pathway leading from one corner of the pool all the way around, ending with steps to the platform. On the day of reckoning, all those charged (Pollywogs) were mustered into the hanger deck by the bears and Police. 'Pollywogs' is a term used in the Navy for all those who have not undergone initiation and who had not yet crossed the Meridian. Here, we were ridiculed and had various things thrown at us, including overripe tomatoes, flour, eggs, jellies, custard, and blancmange. We had our hands tied around our backs and were linked together with a long rope. The rest of the ship's company were mustered on the flight deck. On cue, horns were sounded and the lift from the hanger took us to the flight deck. There was much shouting and jeering and we were marched into position.

The hanger lift descended and more horns were blown. Up from the depth of the hanger came King Neptune, appropriately attired in sacking cloth decorated with seaweed and shells. He had a crown placed upon his head and a trident in his right hand. Accompanying him was his wife, a beautiful 6'2", fifteen-stone beauty who had long flowing locks (made of open hessian rope), breasts covered with sea shells and a tail of canvas. She wore a beard (actually her own) which had been coloured green. She was followed by four burly looking mermaids, all tattooed, equally attired and who probably had more body hair than most mountain gorillas. As the king and his court ascended, the whole ship's company went into overdrive, cheering and whooping, banging an array of homemade instruments and blowing whistles (bosons' calls). The king, queen and the royal court made its way to the platform to take their places for the ceremony. As they walked, the king shouted to the whole ships company, "Oh Err," and the ship's company responded with the same response. The feeling of elation by everyone was awe-inspiring and minute by minute the ship's company was brought to a frenzy.

Once seated, the king ordered, "Read out the charges," appearing from the back of the platform came out the judge. Dressed accordingly as a judge, he mounted the platform. At that, the hanger lift, which had been lowered once again, rose to the flight deck. There, in the middle of the lift, tied to the police stood the captain and the Executive Officer. They were led to the platform with more cries of "Oh Err" and "Oh Err matey". More cheers, whoops and shouting filled the air.

Once on the platform, the Captain was forced to walk the plank and made to sit on the stool at the end.

King Neptune stood and said, "You have been a very naughty boy." Everyone fell about laughing.

"You have bought young land lubbers with you who have been equally as naughty as you. You pollute the seas with this filth. How do you plea?"

"Guilty your Majesty," replied the Captain.

Neptune then turned to the Judge and asked, "What are your findings?"

The Judge said, "Yes, my Lord and King, my findings are that this man has been a very, very naughty boy and as such, must face the consequences."

The Judge turned to the Captain and said, "You have been found guilty on all charges, you must take your punishment."

At that, the King raised his trident and banged it on the platform. Immediately, the bears and police began throwing all of the items we had been covered with whilst in the hanger. They covered the Captain with shaving foam (actually the foam is potato mash) and began to shave him with a grossly oversized cut throat razor made of plywood. They combed his hair with a handmade comb which was at least four-foot long. He was sponged, had buckets of water thrown at him, and made to drink a full pint of beer in one go. Once he had finished his beer, the tankard was taken from him, then he was tipped backwards into the awaiting pool where he was caught by two of the bears. A great cheer arose and everyone clapped. The Captain was dipped underwater like having a baptism, and then lifted out of the pool. The First Officer was next to be led to the platform and the same happened to him. Following the trials of the Captain and First Officer, it was then the turn of Junior Officers and non-commissioned officers to meet their fate, followed by us ratings. After the completion of the ceremony, all those who had been charged, were given a certificate. The certificate or shellback, proclaims and grants the order of the Green Shellback to all those initiated. It provides safe passage to all sailors who sail the seven seas and promises safe passage to the depths should any sailor die at sea.

The ceremony ended and a barbeque was provided for everyone. As you can imagine, the sun was at its height, temperature soaring and beer flowing. Many of the ratings cooled off by jumping into the pool. The 'Airy Fairies' (flight deck crew) rigged up a fire hose which sprayed water like a fountain onto the flight deck to cool those who could not get into the pool. The merriment continued for several hours before being abruptly closed and the flight deck cleared.

A couple of us junior ratings then decided to do a bit of sun bathing. I was joined with Scotty, Jordie and guy called Gallagher. Gallagher was a ginger headed guy and fair skinned. We found an appropriate spot on the 'Bofer' deck (a Bofer is a large gun and part of the ship's armaments). We prepared towels and pillows and began to soak up the equatorial sun. We had all finished our watches and none of us were due back on duty until the following day. After the events of the day, and having drank more than the allocated 'three cans' we all settled down. It wasn't long before we all fell asleep. After a couple of hours in the sun, we began to arouse one by one. Scotty was the first to wake and then woke me and Jordie in turn. When we looked at Gallagher, he had blistered the whole length of his body. His face had ballooned and he moaned as he woke. We could see that he was in tremendous pain and quickly tried to cool him. We helped him to the sickbay so that he could be treated. Gallagher remained in sickbay for four days and was put on a charge of 'self-inflicted' injury. The Captain sentenced Gallagher to 14 days number nine's. Number nine's is a combination of punishments which include a reduction in pay for two weeks, extra hours working and having to muster three times per day outside the Joss's office.

The following day, we arrived at Ascension. Ascension is an isolated volcanic island 7° 56' South of the equator in the South Atlantic. It lies approximately 1,600 kilometres from the coast of Africa and 2,250 kilometres from the coast of Brazil. When we arrived at Ascension, we were not allowed any shore leave. However, the view of the island from the ship was magnificent. Ascension is a British Overseas Territory along with St Helena and Tristan da Cunha. On-board, all of our chefs were of Chinese origin, originating from Hong Kong. The Chinese contingent was naval personnel but could only hold positions on British War Ships as chefs or stewards. Also on board were Chinese civilians who ran the ship's laundry and a clothes shop. The civilian Chinese rarely left their work place or mess so I was surprised to see several of them on top deck. The chefs, stewards and Chinese civilians were all grouped together. They appeared to be having a great time and were busy laughing at an activity they were involved in. On closer inspection, they had attained two metal bread trays. These trays were made of strong wire and had thin ropes attached to each corner of the trays. These ropes were then tied to a central rope creating a pyramid formation. They placed small pieces of bread in the tray and then threw the crate over the side of the ship into the sea. Within minutes, they hauled the tray back up the side of the ship onto the deck. The tray was full of multi-coloured fish. I found later that these were trigger fish. They must have caught 20 or so fish and were excited as these fish were to be their dinner for the evening. In many ways, this was the first time I had recognised cultural difference as fish provided by the navy was nearly always cod and supplied frozen to the ship. Their catch was sufficient to feed them all for several days and I saw later that evening the Chinese guys happily eating their catch.

Two days in Ascension and then we were off again, this time sailing around the Cape of Good Hope. The Cape of Good Hope is a rocky headland on the Atlantic Coast of South Africa. A common misconception is that the Cape of Good Hope is the southern tip of Africa. This misconception was based on the misbelieve that the Cape was the dividing point between the Atlantic and Indian Oceans. The southernmost point of Africa is actually Cape Agulhas which is about 90 miles to the South East. Cape Agulhas is the point where currents of the South Atlantic Ocean meet the warmer waters of the Indian Ocean. That oceanic meeting point fluctuates between Cape Agulhas and Cape Point. As one of the Great Capes of the South Atlantic Ocean, the Cape of Good Hope has long been of special significance to sailors, many of whom refer to it simply as "the Cape". Heading around the cape, we began steaming towards Durban on South Africa's East Coast. We were now in the Indian Ocean and we arrived in Durban on 20 April 1971, where we spent two weeks.

After a month at sea, it was great to be able to relax from the pressure of consistent working. For me, Durban was a special place. Not only was the weather absolutely gorgeous, hot, sunny with gentle breezes, but the city itself was so clean and modern looking. Durban also had the most amazing beaches. Soft golden sands stretched the length of Durban and strategically placed along the beach were brick built barbeques known as Braais (Braai is an Afrikaans word meaning barbeque of grill). Having a Braai on the beach in South Africa is a social event. Many families aim towards the beach each evening and at weekends just to eat and to relax in the warm waters of the Indian Ocean. On 21 April, I along with a couple of other guys decided to visit the beach and enjoy the warm waters too and get in some more sun bathing. Along the coast and about a hundred yards out to sea were large metal nets. These nets were to stop sharks from entering the bathing side and the beach areas. Apparently, Great White Sharks patrolled the area seeking out sardines which frequently gather along this coastline. While we were enjoying our well-earned R&R (rest and relaxation), we were approached by a couple of guys who asked us where we were from. We told them that we from the UK and we were with the Royal Navy and visiting Durban on our way to the Far East. The guys were fascinated and asked us to join them at their Braais with their families. We were treated to steaks, burgers, an array of salads and copious amounts of beer and wine. Elliot and Dan were our inviters and they, along with their wives made excellent company. After spending the day on the beach, we were invited to Elliot's house to continue our R&R. The houses of 'whites' were huge and expensive. All of the larger houses were just for the privileged white population only. The more moderate houses for 'coloureds' (Asian descents) and the shakes for 'blacks', this was the reality of apartheid in South Africa during the 1970s. All white households had black people working for them as gardeners, housekeepers, maids etc. It was a shocking reality and one I really was not comfortable with. The worst thing was that black people were looked down upon by the whites and seen almost as worthless. I was reprimanded when I greeted the gardener and asked how he was. I was told not to talk with the servants. I tried to challenge the attitude of my guests and the way in which they treated their workers, but it was clear that my comments were not welcome. I felt so uneasy that I decided to leave.

"Will we see you tomorrow?" asked Elliot.

"No," I replied. "Tomorrow is my birthday and I have arranged to meet with friends to celebrate."

"Oh wow!" Elliot said. "You must come back here with your friends and we will have a pool party for your birthday."

"Thanks, but no thanks, some of my friends happen to be black and I think that they would feel more uncomfortable than I do."

There was a look of shock on Elliot's face as I said this. I am not sure whether Elliot was shocked because I had admitted to having black friends, whether it was because the UK had black people in our forces, or whether or not he didn't like me saying that I felt uncomfortable. I thanked him and the rest of his group for their hospitality and said that they had been so kind, but I also said that I found their political views quite abhorrent and their attitude to black people quite sickening. I left the house never to return. I was so angry. I knew about apartheid and knew that us 'white ratings' could not mix with our 'black' friends while in South Africa, but to have seen and experienced blatant 'racism' first-hand had been a shocking experience.

The next day was my birthday. Celebrating my seventeenth birthday in Durban was something special, although tinged with sadness. Two of my friends on board were black guys and I could not invite them to celebrate with me. Not only would they not be allowed to enter any of the bars in Durban (reserved for whites only), they were also not allowed to be seen even associating with me. Everything was separated in South Africa at this time. Even down to where you could sit. White park benches were only for 'white people', brown benches for 'coloureds' (Asians) and green benches for 'black people'. Even ambulances were allocated for the different races, the best and newest for 'whites' only. I think that this birthday visit had a profound effect on me and my political views and when we returned to South Africa on our return journey, I was to show my disapproval in a very visible way.

I was now 17 years old and no longer a 'junior' rating. I was now seen as an adult in Navy terms and as such, would be treated as an adult.

My birthday was celebrated with cards from my mess mates and from home. The chefs had baked me a birthday cake, which we ate before breakfast, apart from those who were on watch and they had their share as soon as their watches were over. I spent my day ashore walking around the streets of Durban and spending time on the beach. I had arranged to meet most of my friends later at one of the bars and enjoyed having a wonderful meal at a restaurant I had found during a previous run ashore. My birthday bash would have been something that I would have enjoyed, had I been able to remember it. I certainly know that there were quite a few people in the bar and I know that the drinks were flowing my way. Getting drunk was not the best thing to do on your birthday as it tends to erase all memories. I remember waking the next morning with a dreadful hangover and had at least four bouts of serious vomiting before being able to make sense of the world. My friends said that the evening had been great but all said that it was sad that our black friends couldn't join us.

We spent a further five days in Durban. I made friends with another couple of guys who lived there but like the previous people we had met, their political views were totally opposite to mine. I really struggled with their racist views and the way they spoke to all black and Asian people. Many of the derogatory terms used by them towards the blacks and Asians were in Afrikaans, which meant that

I didn't understand what they were saying but certainly picked up on the sentiment of what they were saying. I thought how arrogant they were but it seemed as all white people were of this ilk.

The black people of Durban were just awesome, many walking proudly and some even dressed in traditional costume. The Zulu people especially were so proud and colourful. The women wore bright colours. They held themselves so straight and proud and gave off an air of importance. I would have loved to have been able to have a conversation with them but even they were bound by the rules of the country. The only real conversation that I had with a black person was when I took a rickshaw. Unlike traditional Chinese rickshaws, the South African rickshaw was highly decorated and was built for speed. The guy who took us was surprisingly chatty and good humoured. Our conversation was more about us than him as he was fascinated by the British and even more so because we were in the Royal Navy. As he took us on our journey, he ran as fast as he could by pulling us behind in our carriage. Then, in order for him to take a rest, he would jump off the ground, get propelled in the air as he held on to the pulling bar and rest before leaning forward to make contact with the road. At the back of the rickshaw, where we were sitting, we were tilted back as the driver rested in the air and the carriage almost touched the road. The ride was exhilarating as well as being fun but also frightening. I cannot remember how many Rand he charged, but I do remember that we paid him extra. I think that maybe he was not used to getting more than the recommended price as he cried out 'Thank you' as loud as he could and kept repeating it.

At the end of April, we left Durban heading for India. We sailed towards Madagascar passing between Madagascar and Mauritius; on past the Seychelles and the Maldives and entering the Arabian Sea and crossing the meridian for the second time travelling north. This time, we did not hold a crossing the line ceremony as no new ratings had joined the ship since our first crossing. We steamed up the West coast of India finally arriving in Bombay (now Mumbai) on 3 May 1971. Mumbai was a vibrant place. At one end of the city was where the affluent people lived. Old colonial houses on wide streets lined with exotic trees and flower beds, at the other side of the city were the slums. Thousands upon thousands of people lived within the slum area (dharavi). The streets were very narrow in the slum areas and raw sewage and water from the houses ran down the streets. Children with little clothing and barefooted ran playing in the filth and rubbish and the smell was difficult to get used to. Many of the houses in the slum areas were just tin shakes or built of old wooden frames covered with tarpaulins, plastic sheeting or made out of mud bricks. The caste system became very evident with the Brahmins (academic and religious leaders) clearly being at the top of the pyramid and the 'Dalits' (the untouchables) at the bottom of the pile. The way in which the system works is based upon a pyramidal structure and has four layers. At the top and above the pyramid are the 'Gods' and below the pyramid and not attached to the main pyramid are the Dalits or untouchables. Within the pyramid structure, the Brahmins sit at the top and below them are the Kshatriyas (the rulers, administrators and warriors) and below these are the Vaishya's (artisans, traders, merchants and farmers) and the Shudras (manual labourers). The untouchables worked on the refuse tip collecting what they could to survive, yet everyone had a smile on their face. Thin dogs searched for scraps, many covered with mange. Life within the slums was hard but small industries kept the people busy. I understand that the informal industries that thrived within Dharavi had an annual turnover nearing 1 billion US dollars. Leather, textiles and pottery goods were produced in vast quantities and you had to admire the entrepreneurship of Dharavi residents. Situated between the affluent area of Mumbai and Dharavi, was the shopping area. Unlike other major cities, all of the shops were small and market stalls lined every street. There was a distinct smell within the shopping area that I can only describe as being like rotting vegetables. Streets were full of people going about their daily business and there were many who lay in the street sleeping. People with disabilities seemed to be everywhere. Many people without limbs or sight; it was amazing to see how these people were able to get about, as there appeared not to be any wheelchairs or such like. Some people had just wooden boards with cabinet wheels attached. They propelled themselves using their hands on the roads. There were many beggars in the streets of Mumbai and even small children would come tapping your legs asking for food or money. I gave some money to one group of children who then decided to adopt me. They followed me everywhere. They laughed as we walked the streets not having a care in the world. I tried to establish where their parents or guardians were, but to no avail. Either they had no adult protection or had been press ganged by cartel groups. It is estimated that three million children are involved in begging in India and that 40,000 children every year are abducted by cartels. Mumbai was not a world that I was used to, but there was something so special about the place that made me want to return many times in later life.

One place that had to be visited was the Gateway of India. The Gateway of India is a monument built in the early twentieth century. It was erected to commemorate the landing in December 1911 at Apollo Bunder, Mumbai (then Bombay) of King George V and Queen Mary the first British monarch to visit India. After its construction, the gateway was used as a symbolic ceremonial entrance to British India for important colonial personnel. It has been called a symbol of "conquest and colonisation" commemorating British colonial legacy. The gateway is also the monument from where the last British troops left India in 1948, following Indian independence. It is located on the waterfront at an angle, opposite the Taj Mahal Palace Hotel and overlooks the Arabian Sea. The Gateway is amongst the prime tourist attractions in Mumbai and also a gathering spot for locals, street vendors, and photographers. Just being at the Gateway gave one the sense that the British had made a considerable impact on India, some believing not necessarily a good impact. However, many locals were happy to see British naval personnel wondering around and came over to greet us.

We also visited the 'Cages', not to participate but just to see just how busy these amenities were. The 'Cages' are the notorious side of Mumbai where teenage girls who had been trafficked; are held in cages for month and potentially years to work as prostitutes. The madams would keep the girls like slaves in the cages until they were "broken", to the extent that they would not try to run away. The girls were only ever taken out to eat or to be given to a customer for sex. It was a poor, sad place to visit and there were literally hundreds of young girls there living in squalor and poverty. I would imagine that disease was rife in this awful place, as at that time, there was no sign of medical intervention and the girls were seen as disposable commodities.

It was with mixed feelings I re-joined my ship getting ready to depart for the Far East. On the day we left Mumbai, I celebrated my first full year since joining the navy. I had not regretted one single second of my decision to join the navy even though I had begun to see things happening around the world that often caused me pain and anxiety, but overall, my time in the navy thus far had been amazing.

Chapter Six
My Spiritual Home

Sailing south, we left the Arabian Sea, circumnavigated the Laccadive Sea around Sri Lanka and entered the Indian Ocean once more. We sailed the southern end of the Bay of Bengal eastward towards Malaysia and Singapore. After a passage of seven weeks from Portsmouth, HMS Albion embarked 40 Commando Royal Marines off Changi in Singapore before actually docking in Singapore. The ship and Royal Marines were first set to engage on an exercise as a counter-terrorist operation in Brunei. Brunei is a tiny nation on the island of Borneo, in two distinct sections surrounded by Malaysia and the South China Sea. At that time, the UK had responsibilities for the external affairs and defence of Brunei and had a close relationship with the Sultan. The exercises went well and were completed on time with maximum effect. On completion of this exercise, the ship entered Singapore waters. We held a ceremonial entry into Singapore (procedure Alpha) and 848 squadron provided an impressive flypast as the air squadron disembarked to HMS Sembawang. We docked in Sembawang docks for a month for an Assisted Maintenance Period (AMP). An AMP allows for the ship's company to complete repairs and do maintenance to a ship whilst at the same time will have support from Naval Dockyard personnel.

On our arrival at Singapore, I was transferred from my Auxiliary stoker duties to the boiler rooms. POME Hughes was in charge of my watches and his idea of training was to throw you into the deep end. No standing around taking in your surroundings, learn by doing was his motto. My first task was to help empty the boilers of their water and clean the inside of each boiler taking away any build-up of rust and checking that pipe work was sound. We also had to clean out the fire pit (the area where the oil burners focused their heat to boil the water in the lower boilers). Any repairs to the inside of the boilers are carried out while the boilers are in their cold state. Further, all of the external pipe work within the boiler room had to be checked and replacement valves put in where wear or damage had made them inefficient. This meant removing all lagging from the pipes and re-lagging after the work was complete. We also had to change the burners within the fire areas and remove the clinker that had built over time. These jobs were to take the full month in Singapore and had to be completed for the designated sailing date.

Our daily routine of coving watches changed into a nine to five working day. So from 0900 to 1700, we worked completing the tasks set. Crawling into these large boilers was rather difficult to say the least and those who had larger builds struggled to get inside. Once inside, we were expected to brush the inside of each boiler with a wire brush until the surface of the boilers had changed from a rusty brown to something that resembled a more metallic colour, after which, the boiler could be fully checked over and joints and pipes removed or repaired. We worked in these confined places for weeks, getting filthy every day. Removing the clinker from the fire area was similar, in that we had to chip off clinker build up with handheld chipping mallets then shovel the waste into buckets before removing the waste from the fire area and boiler room. While in the fire area, we had to remove the burners and the sprayers, replacing them with new, more efficient burners. We then had to start on the stripping of the cladding which surrounded the multitude of pipes coming into and out of the boiler rooms. Many of these pipes were six inches plus in diameter and were lagged with asbestos. Getting rid of the asbestos was a task in itself. We sawed, cut, chipped and broke the asbestos to uncover the metal pipe work, then after, repaired and replacing worn valves, having to recover the pipe work with new asbestoses. This was all done by hand, from the mixing of dry asbestos with water in buckets to smoothing a thick layer of asbestos around each and every pipe. The pipes also had to have an outer dressing, much like bandaging a broken limb. Yard upon yard of Asbestos bandage was wrapped around the internal core of asbestos, and then smoothed to give an aesthetic look. Each pipe doubled in size as the asbestos was applied. Once dry, we had to paint the asbestos white and stencil on the pipes what was going through them; i.e. steam, oil, water and apply an arrow giving the direction of flow. After all, the ship had started life in 1944, launched in 1947 and commissioned in 1954 and was one of the older ships in the British Royal Fleet and needed some attention. Although the ship had undergone many refits and AMP's during her life, she needed extra loving care to ensure that she would fulfil her motto of ***Fortiter, Fideliter, Feliciter*** (Boldly, Faithfully, Successfully) and to continue to serve the British Royal Navy.

Singapore was and remains a very special place in my mind, not just because of the AMP and all of the hard work we had to put into getting the ship battle ready, but because of the many friends I made there. I just loved this country. Singapore is warm and tropical all year around. Rainfall when it comes is heavy, warm and short-lived. The average temperature due to its maritime position is 31 degrees during the daytime and 25 degrees at night. Its relative humidity ranges between 70–80 percent, meaning that day or night, it is warm and sticky. Our first run ashore went no further than the NAAFI (or the Dockyard club as it was known) located within Sembawang Dock Yard. The NAAFI boasted not only a really good shop but also a vibrant bar and restaurant and swimming pool. It was a relaxing place to meet up with friends and also a place for quiet reflection and relaxation. As you might have guessed, because of the warmth of the weather and the stickiness caused by the humidity, we aimed for the swimming pool to cool off. This first run ashore included some of the guys from my mess who had never gone ashore together before. One of the guys 'Jock', who had joined us for the first time turned out to be a barrel of fun. We spent so much time in the water splashing around that we almost forgot that we had to get back to the ship. As a result, we ran through the dockyard in flip flops and our swimming trunks. On arriving at the ship, we were not allowed back on board until we had fully dressed. We had a full two minutes to dress appropriately and to run up the gang way. Had we been a second over our given time, we would have been placed on a charge and would have had our privileges removed. We ran back to the mess laughing and planning our first proper run ashore the following day.

After duties, Jock, Jordie, Scotty and I all made our way into Sembawang village. Leaving the dockyard gate I distinctly remember the heady smell of jasmine in the air. As we walked out of the dockyard, shops, bars, eating places and a brothel faced us. On the side of the dockyard stood a tall iron fence which surrounded the whole of the dockyard. In front of this fence running parallel was a monsoon ditch. The ditch was about six-foot-deep and four-foot-wide. We had been warned to keep well away from the monsoon ditches as when dry, they were home to rats and snakes (some of which were venomous). When flooded, the waters raged towards the outlet near the estuary. The torrent of water could be so strong that if you fell in, you would be washed away very quickly. I was told that some people had died after falling in. We wandered across the road looking into the shops, many selling modern electrical goods and jewellery. There were lots of places to eat both indoors and outside and then there was the brothel. As we passed the brothel, we were invited in by the 'Momma San' at the door. We all smiled and giggled, passing comments (which were not offensive) but declined her invitation. After all, it was early evening, the sun had not gone down and we were not about to give good money away on our first trip out. Another reason for turning down the Momma San's invitation was because we had also been warned on board about the dangers of engaging in sexual exploits especially in brothels. We had been educated in sexually transmitted disease whilst we were at sea and shown explicit film footage of the ravages of gonorrhoea (the clap), non-specific urethritis (nob rot) and syphilis (the pox). Next door to the brothel was an open market area selling all sorts of exotic fruit, vegetables, meat and fish, which after dark, converted to outdoor restaurants. We had arrived at that time of day when the conversion was just taking place. We wandered the market chatting to the locals. The warmth of the locals was overwhelming and it seemed as if everyone wanted us to stop and chat with them. Before leaving the market, we had to promise that we would return later to have a late night meal and a final drink before returning to the ship.

Singapore's population is made up of indigenous Malayans, Chinese and Indians with a number of expats (British) who tended to live further towards the city centre. One of the restaurant owners was Mohammed who was supported by his young ten-year-old son Hussein. It was Hussein who was insistent that we return to his restaurant for food later, and he who kept on telling us that his father's food was the best in Singapore.

The shops and bars in Sembawang were reminiscent to bars in old Wild West movies, raised higher than the road way and which had wide wooded walkways between them. Most of the shops sold electrical items such as radios, cassette players, TVs, binoculars and such, other shops sold gold jewellery, precious gems and watches. There was a tailor's shop and shoe shop where you could have clothes and shoes made to measure, a Chinese silk shop which sold exotic embroidered dresses, pictures and porcelain. The bars were inter-dispersed. None of the bars had windows but displayed their name in neon above their doorways.

As it was hot, we chose one of the bars to make our first visit. As we went through the door of the bar, we could smell incense burning and the perfume wafted through the bar in waves. The actual bar was situated at the far end and was being cleaned by the barman who gave a smile and nodded in recognition that we were there. Sitting at the bar were four young women who smiled and shouted "hewow (hello) boys, come in, come in, have good time, we look after you."

Tables were set to the left and right and there was a clear walkway to the bar. As we walked towards the bar, two of the girls jumped up from their stools and ushered us towards a table. As the door closed, the bar became quite dark and it was difficult to see in the subdued lighting. We ordered four cold Tiger beers which were served at the table. One girl 'Gina' pulled a chair over to our table and joined us.

"You young boy's huh. You buy me sticky green, only one dollar?"

(A Singapore Dollar was at that time equivalent to two shillings and four pence English currency). None of us had a clue what a 'sticky green' was, but as we didn't have to drink it, we thought why not and paid Gina her one dollar. Gina was served with a very small glass of some green substance. We thought that it must be Crème de menthe or something similar. Later we found that it was nothing more than a small glass of lime squash which possibly cost only two pence. Yes, we had been 'ripped off' but at least Gina and the barman got a cut and added money to their very minimal weekly wage. Gina drank up and moved her chair to be closer to us. Electricity in Sembawang was sporadic, so every now and again all of the lights would go out and everything was thrown into darkness. While we sat, one of the frequent power cuts occurred. The next thing we found that there was someone under the table trying to molest us all, taking in turn to grab our groins.

"Wow, wow, wow, slow down love," we all cried almost in unison, "what the hell! We've only come in for a drink!"

Out from under the table crawled another of the young women.

"You don't want Rosie?"

"No thanks love, it's very kind of you but this is our first run ashore and this is the first bar we have been in."

Rosie walked away dejected and muttering something in Malay or Mandarin Chinese that was inaudible to us all. We ordered another drink, talked about the invasion of our privacy and laughed at our first experience of Singapore. The electricity went off again and we had a repartition of the previous power cut.

"For god's sake," Jock said. "Not again, get out of it ya dirty bastard."

To our even greater surprise, it was not Rosie this time, but the barman.

"Fuck sake," said Jock, "they're all fuckin perverts in here, let's go."

We left our drinks and the bar in double quick time, but could not stop laughing at our experience. Jock had taken the experience to heart and was quite angry. I think he was more embarrassed than angry but soon saw the funny side of the incident.

We walked the length of Sembawang and decided to try to find Nisoon, a small district just outside of Sembawang. We had been told that Nisoon held a night market and was a place that we should visit. As it was now dusk, we began walking asking direction along the way. We managed to reach Nisoon but didn't find the market. On asking, we were told the market was only held on Wednesdays and as it was Sunday, we were out of luck. Having walked this far, we decided to descend on the local bars where we were joined by more of the ships company. By 2300 hours, we were well and truly inebriated; one of the guys who had been to Singapore before told us that he was going to 'Jonny Ghurkhas' and invited us along. 'Jonny Ghurkha' turned out to be a tattooist and most naval personnel had visited his shop on more than one occasion. We accompanied our friend to the tattoo parlour and watched as he chose the tattoo he wanted. We watched as a transfer was made onto thin paper and then applied to his leg. The outline of the tattoo formed a dragon and reached from the guys' knee to almost his ankle. We watched with awe as Jonny drew the outline with black ink and then how he skilfully, coloured the dragon, adding shade and form as he went along. None of us who were with him had a tattoo at that stage, but it certainly set a seed in all of our heads. We all ended up getting tattoos before we left Singapore, but that is another story. Jonny Ghurkha was a skilled artist and the colours and shading he applied were first rate. The dragon looked beautiful. After completing the tattoo, Jonny applied Vaseline all over his work and covered the tattoo with thin gauze, after which he taped the gauze with Elastoplast tape.

After our evening out in Nisoon, we hailed a taxi back to Sembawang, had a drink in one of the bars but avoided the bar we had been earlier then went for 'Big eats' at the market restaurant. Hussein immediately saw us entering the market area and ran over to greet us.

"Please, please, come sit down. My dad does best food in market, you'll love it, you can have steak, fish, curry, we have everything, my dad cook it, come sit here."

We sat at a table and Hussein ran to get the menu. He placed glasses, knives, forks and spoons on the table, flicking the spoils of the last visitor's meal onto the dirt floor.

Chicken soup was on the starter menu. I thought that this was going to be homemade and so I plumbed for the soup followed by chicken satay. The chicken soup came and to my surprise, it was out of tin, heated to boiling in a wok and served with fresh crusty bread. From then on, every time I returned to Hussein's restaurant, I began my meal with chicken soup. The chicken satay was phenomenal, the best that I had ever tasted and a start to my culinary explorations. Singapore has an array of street food venues and is rich in variety; Malay, Chinese, South Indian and English cuisine available day and night. There was even a Fish and Chips van outside the dockyard gate and for just one dollar you were served with chips and a choice of fish, pies, sausage and kebabs. The favourite of most was King Prawn and Chips. The King prawns were as large as a pork loin chop, were hot and juicy and tasted so fresh, dipped in a crunchy batter and with tartar sauce on the side. Another favourite was Chicken Marmme. This was broiled chicken with noodles, served in a broth with scallions and spices. For a quick snack, there was barbequed ham. The ham looked like shaped boiled ham, which was brushed with honey and grilled on charcoal. These flavours still resonate in my mouth as I write. Singapore's food market in the centre of Singapore City still remains one of the best places in the world for exquisite food at a very low price. All food had to be washed down with Tiger Beer, the local beer of the region.

The following Wednesday, we managed to get to Nisoon Night Market. This market held hundreds of stalls selling everything imaginable. The market was brightly lit with power coming from small generators. The market stretched along a dirt road which ran for about a mile with stalls on either side. It seemed as if the whole of Singapore's residents were there and the bustle of people shopping for bargains added to the excitement. It seemed as if everyone in Singapore had been on happy drugs, there was not one miserable face to be seen anywhere. The smiling faces of people were infectious; *how could anyone not enjoy themselves at this amazing market?* After buying stuff from the market that we didn't really need we made our way back to Sembawang. After taking a few drinks in one or two of the bars, we began to walk back. We noticed one or two of the ship's company filing out of the brothel at the far end. Of course they had been drinking heavily and all appeared satisfied with what had been on offer.

Several days later, we saw the same guys coming out of sickbay. All had contracted Gonorrhoea. Not only did they have the preverbal discharge and stinging when urinating, all were restricted to the ship and all taking copious amounts of antibiotics. It was, as a result of seeing those guys, which provided me with a lesson to learn. "Don't do brothels and avoid becoming a member of the 'clap' group." The lessons of others I learned very quickly and made sure that I would never become a member of this group.

We had the weekend off and so six of us planned to go into Singapore city to see the highlights. The main attraction for all visitors was Bugis Street. Bugis Street was a street market during the day selling fruit, vegetables, meat and fish, by night; it was converted to outdoor restaurants and bars. This twenty-four hour explosion of entertainment was something to behold. I had been told that I would love Bugis street and that Bugis street would love me. Little did I know just how much I would love this place and how I would become a 'special' item, revered by the people who ran the street.

Friday evening, we travelled by taxi to the centre of Singapore and booking a hotel room in Baliaster Street. Baliaster Street is one of the main thorough fares through Singapore's shopping area; it is close to Little India and China Town and of course Bugis Street. Opposite the hotel stood a Buddhist Temple and about twenty yards away a Hindu Temple; on the other side and about the same distance away from the Buddhist Temple stood a Catholic Church. Such is Singapore, catering for every belief system and every denomination of those religions.

We were all excited about going to Bugis street and the older guys who had been to Singapore previously appeared more excited that us 'greens' (greens referred to younger ratings with little experience or knowledge; also known as Sproggs). When we arrived in Bugis street, the restaurants and bars were in full swing. The street was adorned with beautiful women, all seemed to be linked to one of the restaurant/bars. The older guys greeted the women as we walked through and many knew each other on first name terms. We eventually found a table and ordered beers.

Suddenly, out of nowhere came this very tall blonde woman wearing pink tinted sunglasses. "Hello darlings, Hi James, Hi Pete, so good to have you back," the woman said. "Who have you bought with you this time? I see you have bought me a lovely 'Cherry boy.'"

The older guys laughed.

"This is young Brummie, Jock, Jordie, Tim and Tansy," James replied. "Guys, this is Big Angie."

Angie did appear big for a woman, standing about 6'3" tall, with broad shoulders, very large hands and quite a gruff voice.

Angie nodded, walked towards me and said, "You are all pretty boys but you, (touching my head), you are especially pretty. You can be my Cherry Boy."

"What's a Cherry Boy?" I asked.

James, Pete and Big Angie burst into fits of laughter.

"A Cherry Boy is a virgin, someone who has not lost their virginity, has not had their cherry popped yet," Angie said very seriously.

James and Pete laughed even louder, hardly containing themselves.

"You be my Cherry Boy, Angie will look after you."

"Oh my god," said Pete, "you're highly honoured. Kaytai's (pronounced KyeTie), really look after their Cherry Boys and it seems that you have taken the fancy of Big Angie."

I was then informed that all the 'Girls' on Bugis Street were Transgender men and that they held the cartel in Bugis Street.

"Don't worry," said James, "she doesn't want your body; she just wants to show you off."

For some reason, it was prestigious for a Kaytai to have a Cherry Boy. Cherry Boys were revered, especially if you were European.

Big Angie walked between the tables greeting people, making people laugh with sexual innuendo and occasionally disappearing with some American Guy. Angie kept returning to our table to check that we were all OK and paid special attention to me. She came over at one stage, pushed a 50 dollar note in my tee shirt as said, "You buy Angie drink. Only Fanta Orange, no alcohol."

I did as requested and presented the drink to Big Angie.

She said, "You keep change; you buy Angie drink when she is thirsty."

This turned out to be a great deal, Angie gave me money to buy her drinks, I kept the change, which was around 40 dollars, which paid for my taxi back to the hotel and provided me with drinks too. We headed back to the hotel in the early hours, content with our evening out and looked forward to the next two days.

Saturday, after getting up late, we made our way to Changi, where we spent time on the beach. Changi was also home to the famous Changi Prison, a place used by the Japanese during WWII, built by the British during the 1930s it was known as the best prison facility in the British Empire. However, during the occupation, Changi became a death camp with thousands being incarcerated as prisoners of war. Many people died of starvation at this prison. Over 500 women were detained in Changi, separated from the men and their children. The atrocities carried out in Changi are well-documented and remains a place of pilgrimage in honour of those who either died or were killed here at the hands of the Japanese. Later in the afternoon, we browsed the shops in China Town. China Town is adorned with mythical Tigers and Dragons and many of the properties are painted vibrant red and gold. The Chinese community living in Singapore also provide entertainment and carnivals celebrating Chinese New Year and Buddhist religious days. China Town is filled with shops bars and restaurants. After having 'Big eats', we returned to the hotel where we rested for a short time, then changed and made our way back to Bugis Street.

Big Angie had reserved a table for us and as well as drinking the night away, we also people watched. It was surprising to see just how well the Kaytai's managed the area. Any troublemakers were quickly dealt with and expulsed from the area by gangs of Chinese men who remained on the periphery. Whilst sitting there, someone tapped me on my back.

"It's about time you got the drinks in you tight fisted fucker," a voice from behind said.

It was notable that this voice had a very strong Black Country accent. I turned and to my astonishment, there stood David Williams. Dave had been a school friend and I had not seen Dave since leaving school. Dave informed me that he had joined the Royal Marines at around the same time as I had joined the navy. Coincidentally, Dave's grandmother and my mother had been friends too. It is a shock when you travel half way around the world only to bump into someone you know well. Dave joined us and after brief introductions to the rest of the gang, Dave and I gave an account of our movements since leaving school. Dave was stationed in Sembawang barracks and would be joining HMS Albion prior to its next sailing. Dave was heading back to barracks at the end of the night but we agreed to meet each other again next time when we were in Bugis Street. It is funny that the saying 'It's a small world' sprang to mind.

We spent Sunday wandering around Little India. Little India houses some of the most beautiful and colourful Hindu temples I have ever seen, adorned with hundreds of statues of Hindu deity. These temples resembled step pyramids and the statues painted in multicolours. Outside each of the temples were places where flower garlands could be purchased. The majority of flowers were marigolds strung together, with the occasional red or white rose placed like jewels in a necklace. Incense was burned outside of the temples which gave off a heady smell of sandalwood. It is funny, but every time I think of Singapore, the smell of jasmine always enters my nostrils. Jasmine grew everywhere, like weeds as did Singapore Orchids. While we walked through Little India, I bought a box of orchids and had them sent home to my mother. I recall my mother being gobsmacked by the amount and variety of orchids she received. She told me much later that the orchids lasted for weeks. Some she flower-pressed and which she kept for years.

Days in Singapore went slowly in many ways but far too quickly in retrospect. Our next outing was to Nisoon market the following week. We drank far too much and ended up in Johnny Ghurkhas. My first tattoo was of a small swallow with a ribbon in its beak and the word mother written on the ribbon. This was engraved on my right forearm. I am not sure if I had chosen this small tattoo because it was my first and I had been afraid of the pain to be inflicted or whether I didn't have enough money to pay for a larger tattoo. Anyway, I returned to Johnny Ghurkhas the following week to have another tattoo on my left forearm. This was a memorial to my father who had died when I was aged 11. Because the tattoo on my left arm was bigger than the one on my right arm, I had a third tattoo, a rose, place under the swallow, evenly matching my tattoos. A forth tattoo was done by Jonny on our next visit to Singapore showing my allegiance to the Royal Navy and to England. It seemed all naval ratings had tattoos of some nature and many had gained them in Singapore and Hong Kong.

After our one month in Singapore and following the AMP. We embarked the Australian Army Band, the ship then sailed out of Singapore at the end of June heading for Japan. During this outward journey we encountered typhoons in the South China Sea. We also carried out full-power trials to make sure that the repairs we had done had been efficiently carried out. To our surprise, we actually made some of the fastest speeds ever recorded by HMS Albion since her first sea trials in 1954. Sailing towards Japan we entered the South China Sea, the Philippine Sea, the Pacific Ocean and the East China Sea. Passing Cambodia, Vietnam, Macau, Hong Kong, China and Taiwan.

Chapter Seven
Land of the Golden Sun
and into the Jungle

During the first leg of our journey, in the South China Sea, we completed our sea trials and began steaming steadily towards Japan to the coastal port of Kobe. One evening not long after we had left Singapore, and off the coastline of Vietnam, I decided to take a walk on one of the upper decks. I was alone, standing and looking out to sea. What was so amazing on this evening was that the sea was dead calm, almost flat and without even a ripple on its surface. I was suddenly joined by one of the officers on board who asked what I was doing.

"Nothing sir," I replied. "I'm just fascinated by how calm the sea is. It's like glass, hardly a ripple. Bit scary really."

"You're very observant," the officer replied, apparently and unbeknown to me, this officer was the meteorological officer. "You have heard it said, there's always calm before a storm?" he asked.

"Yes," I replied.

"Well, we are heading towards some pretty bad weather, typhoons to be exact. We will be battening the hatches soon and things are going to get very rough. I hope that you are not prone to sea sickness?" he said smiling.

"No sir, I did quite well in the Bay of Biscay, in the Arctic and around the Cape too. Better than some who couldn't keep a meal down," I said.

I then relayed a story of when we were in the Arctic and a time I had walked through the Galley during my duties. People trying to eat their meals and their meal trays had slid off the tables and some were throwing up.

"Well…" the officer said, "It's going to be a bit like that but probably a little bouncier," and it was.

When the typhoon hit, it felt as if all hell had been let loose. However, the 'The Old Grey Ghost' steadfastly kept to her course and drove straight through.

After the Typhoon, the weather improved and there were no more scary weather conditions to contend with.

HMS Albion was in Kobe from 1–8 July 1971. Docking in Japan was like a dream coming true. I had always wanted to visit this country even though I had heard that the Japanese held some very peculiar customs. Japan is a fascinating country and the people tightly bound to cultural tradition. Their etiquette not only prescribes courteous behaviour and respect, but expects everyone to abide by their codes of practice. Everyone we met would bow, not just once, but a copious amount of times in greeting. As visitors to Japan, the authorities had granted us free visits to 'Bath Houses', Tea Rooms and to cultural centres. Food in Japan is totally different to the rest of Far Eastern cuisine. Fish was a main element of their diet and lots of sticky rice. Much of the fish was prepared raw and everything appeared to have wasabi paste added to it. Wasabi is a paste made of a radish type vegetable and leaves a hot tingling sensation on the tongue. Food is often dipped in a soya based sauce often laced with ginger and chillies. The food was hard to get use to and because we had to use chop sticks, we became quite efficient very quickly. Interestingly enough, the chop sticks used by the Japanese are much thinner than those used by the Chinese, and tend to be much more pointed on the eating end.

Kobe is a city situated in Osaka Bay in central Japan. It is a very scenic place surrounded by mountains. Mount Rokko is the largest of the surrounding mountains and a great view of Kobe can be had by going to its summit. On the other side of the mountain, outdoor hot spring can be found in Arima Onsen. These springs are warmed by volcanic action deep beneath the ground and are a favourite place to obtain relief from joint pains and arthritis. Kobe boasts one of the oldest Japanese Shinto shrines dating back to the third century. Our trip up to the mountains and to the hot springs was awe-inspiring. Never had I seen a more beautiful pristine place. The air was clean, so too were all of the roads and other facilities. The politeness of the people was humbling and to think, it had only been just over 25 years since Japan was defeated in WWII. You gained a sense that the Japanese were still mourning their defeat and appeared apologetic in everything that they did for us as guests. There were no mad runs ashore in Japan. Yes, we had a few beers and drank warm Sake, but it was if we had become reverent to the Japanese people and their situation.

On the second day ashore, we visited Takarazuka, which is based on the Muko river. We caught a train from Kobe to Amagasaki, then transferred to a

88

train to Takarazuka; the journey taking just over an hour. Trains in Japan are always on time, leaving stations on the exact second. Trains always arrived at their destination at the precise time too. All Japanese trains are immaculately clean, both inside and out. The Japanese rail system also doesn't skimp on luxury for passengers. Seats were quite luxurious and it felt as if you were sitting in an arm chair. I remember thinking that British rail could learn much from the Japanese.

Takarazuka is located in Hyōgo Prefecture and boasts an all women theatre group and the city streets are lined with cherry blossom trees. Apparently, lesbianism in Japan arose from Takarazuka. At the time of visiting, trees had lost their blossom and we didn't have time to visit the famous theatre there. However, the city was hosting a cultural week in the main park. Takarazuka is famed for its municipal parks, including the rose garden. The festival consisted of a mock-up of a Samurai Village and depicted Japanese life before opening up to Western influences. Houses, gardens, farming activities, Shinto shrines, a dōjō and art studios were meticulously reconstructed and presented as a living museum. The whole experience was fascinating and you felt as if you had been taken back in time. There were displays of Japanese Noh, Kabuki and Kyōgen theatre all accompanied by Hayashi musicians. Noh and Kabuki are traditional styles of Japanese theatre and although the performances were lost to us Brits, the spectacle was quite mind-blowing. Kyōgen is comical and used puppets, similar to our Punch and Judy but far more sophisticated. I would have been happy to stay there for a week at least but unfortunately we only had a day at this magnificent festival. I purchased a few items to bring home with me including some very highly lacquered chopsticks in a presentation box, decorative fans that I had seen being made and a Sake (rice wine) set. All were carefully preserved and given as presents when I returned to the UK.

The following day a group of us took up the invitation of Kobe's hospitality to visit one of their many bath houses. Arriving at the bath house, we were greeted by a woman dressed in Geisha attire wearing fully Geisha makeup. The woman bowed muttering some greeting and moving us toward a changing room. The woman looked like a porcelain doll, perfect in every sense of the word. Not a hair out of place, not a crease in her costume and her makeup exquisitely applied. The Japanese do not make direct eye contact and see this as being quite rude. For us Westerners, this caused some embarrassment as within our culture eye contact is seen as a 'normal' cultural value. The embarrassment was because we just didn't know where to look or how to respond. In the dressing room, we were greeted by other women wearing traditional robes but who did not wear the makeup of a geisha. Something was said by the women who had met us at the door and the other women began tittering. All of the women covered their mouths with their hand and stared at the floor. Then each of the women took us singularly to an open cubicle. There, they proceeded to undress us. They maintained our dignity by placing a robe around our shoulders and before removing our underwear placed towels around our waists. We were discouraged from helping in anyway shape or form. When we were all ready, we were taken to a sauna, where our robes were removed and encouraged to sit with quite a few Japanese men who politely acknowledged our presence. There was a television in the sauna and the Japanese men were engrossed in watching the programme on screen. As none of my group could speak Japanese, we hadn't a clue what was going on. We tried to have a conversation amongst ourselves but it was clear that this was not an appropriate thing to do. Nothing was said but the look on the Japanese guys' faces said it all. After some time, a door at the opposite end of the sauna opened and the women who had undressed us urged us to follow them. The women had changed their attire and were now wearing tee shirts and shorts. We were taken into a large room that contained two pools. One was small but could accommodate around ten people and the other large. I would imagine that at least 50 people could have fitted around the periphery with plenty of space to spare. The larger of the pools had a waterfall cascading over rocks down the far side and there were a number of men sitting in the pool having quiet conversation. Around the edge of the room, small stools were located. Each of the stools had a mirror, shower head and a small table, on which stood an array of cleaning products. We were led to the smaller of the two pools and the women removed our towels and encouraged us to get in. The water was absolutely freezing. The shock of the cold water after coming out of the sauna was akin to being hit all over with a sledge hammer. As you might imagine, none of us stayed in this pool very long. After much laughing by everyone within this room, we got out and were given our towels back. We were then led to one of the stools and sat facing the mirror. There, the girl who had been allocated to us promptly began to wash us. Starting with our hair then sponging our upper bodies, legs and feet. We were encouraged to wash our own private parts. After washing, we were showered, taken to the large pool and plunged into hot water. The whole experience was not only relaxing but quite refreshing. After about half an hour, we were taken from the pool back to our allocated stools. We were dried thoroughly with warm towels, massaged with warm oils, were given a manicure and pedicure and our hair brushed. We were then given clean robes to wear. Leading us out of the wash area, we were taken into another small cubicle which consisted cushions and a very low coffee table. After sitting down on one set of cushions, our allocated girl left the room. Within ten minutes, our girl returned dressed in the kimono that she had worn when we arrived. She sat opposite, clapped her hands and another woman come into the room and presented the girl sitting with items to be used in the tea ceremony. The precision to which the tea was prepared and presented was quite emotional. I had never felt such respect from anyone at this level before. After drinking our tea, each of us that had attended was taken back into the changing room and to the cubicle where we had undressed. All of our clothes had been washed, dried and pressed then folded on a table ready for us to wear. Even our shoes had been polished. Before being dressed, we were splashed with sweet scented water akin to aftershave, but far more subtle. As we sat waiting, our respective girls then lit a cigarette and passed it to us. We didn't even have to take the cigarette out of our mouths, this was done for us. After dressing, the girl bowed lowly and muttered something which I can only guess at being a farewell. We were then led out of the building. As you can imagine, the conversation between the guys was focused purely on the experience that we had all gone through and how clean and refreshed we all felt. Never in my life have I ever felt so clean and uplifted.

One of the guy said, "Well that was like the best sex ever without actually having sex. I'm content and if I die tomorrow, I'll die happy."

There was something spiritual about being in Japan and although the streets, bars and restaurants were very busy, you always felt relaxed and at peace with the world. Unfortunately, our trip to Japan was short-lived and we departed Japan with a sad heart but we were happy in the knowledge that we were returning to Singapore.

Learning in the Royal Navy is ongoing. After leaving the UK Junior ratings had been encourage to learn all of the mechanical systems on board ship. We had been provided with paper information, books and exercise books to record our learning. Somehow, the trip to Japan had spurred me to try and complete as much as I could possibly do while at sea and to be promoted from the rank of MEM2 to MEM1. I had moved into the older ratings mess from the junior mess, had attained my MEM status from JMEM and now I wanted to gain a star above my propeller, which was the emblem for Stokers. I studied hard sailing from Japan to Singapore and sat in my spare time writing up my knowledge. Part of the assessment was to provide technical drawings of each system. These had to be drawn to scale, depicted in colour and had to have a key showing what each colour represented, i.e. 'blue' for water, 'red' for steam, 'brown' for oil etc. By the time we had reached Singapore, I had completed all of the tasks that had been set.

"You've worked really hard," said my chief.

"Yes, I call it the Japan effect."

I then had to explain to the chief what I meant by this.

"I totally get you," the chief said. "It's amazing how a visit to each country will have an effect on you personally. I just hope that you will get something from each country we visit."

My work was assessed, marked and then I was invited to take a 'viva voce' (oral examination). Mission accomplished, I made the grade and was promoted to MEM1, and I gained my star and then had to remove all of my arm badges from my dress uniforms, tropical gear, number eight's and overalls, replacing them with the starred propeller. My wages were increased but most of all, the respect and prestige of others also increased. My next aim would be to become a Leading Hand (Killick). Life at sea was my heaven. *Who could wish for a better life?* I had everything I needed, was travelling to far off exotic places, held a responsible job and felt so secure. I was also particularly happy because we were going back to Singapore. I loved this place so much. I felt at home here and wallowed in the fact that the climate actually suited me down to the ground. On arriving at Singapore, the marines were preparing to undergo jungle training. We had just taken on board a company from the Ghurkha regiment and together, the marines and Ghurkha's would embark on a three-day exercise.

I was fascinated with the Ghurkha's. They were all short in stature, had an air of devotion about them, were always immaculately turned out, but tended not to socialise with anyone other than their own regiment. I was spellbound when seeing them clean their equipment, nothing was overlooked and when they cleaned their Ghurkha knives they polished them until it resembled a mirror. At the handle end of a Ghurkha knife (Kukri) is a small sharp 'W' cut into the metal blade. Each time the Ghurkha's removed their blades from their scabbard, they would nick their thumbs on this sharp edge to draw blood. They then wiped the blood along the length of the blade before polishing it. I was told that Ghurkha's are not allowed to draw their knives without drawing blood. The kukri or khukuri is a type of machete originating from the Indian subcontinent, and is traditionally associated with the Nepali-speaking Ghurkhas of Nepal and India. The knife has a distinct re-curve in its blade. Each Ghurkha's thumb had become knarred to clean their knives; through repetitive cutting of their thumbs. Even when they were eating I could not keep my eyes off them. When any of the ship's company or marines had their meals, they would take one of the metal trays and in each compartment would separate starters from their main meals and keep puddings and deserts separately too. Not so the Ghurkhas. They would just pile starters, main course and desert onto their trays without distinguishing the different courses. They ate with gusto, never leaving anything to be thrown away. They were never wasteful. After only two days in Singapore, the marines and Ghurkhas were ready to be flown off the ship to their respective training camps. An invitation was made to any of the ship's company who was interested, to join in this exercise. Just because I could and because I fancied doing something out of the ordinary, I put my name forward. Luckily, I was picked to go with the marines and after packing the required gear, joined the marines to be flown into Jahor Bahru. Jahor is a state in southern Malaysia linked to Singapore by causeways. Jahor is known for its rainforests. Near to Jahor city lies Gunung Pulai, a high hill. It is regarded as a mountain by the Malay people because the name 'Gungan' means mountain although it strictly isn't high enough to be classed a mountain. What is special about this area is that it contains substantial primary rainforests and a spectacular waterfall. The forest was home to Gibbons, Tapirs, Civets and barking deer. Invertebrates were abundant, including Nymph butterflies as well as pitcher plants that grew along tracks and roads. We flew into Jahor aboard Wessex five helicopters and were landed in a small clearing in the deeper part of the rainforest. There we had to set up a base camp for the next few days' exercise. Marines busied themselves with tasks that they seemed used to doing and us naval ratings did jobs that we were told to do. We mainly helped setting up the officer's quarters, the food tent and making latrines. All were hard work but also tinged with fun elements. After all, this was not just an exercise, but to us naval personnel, it was an adventure. Each of the naval personnel was then attached to smaller groups of marines who had the added task of looking after us. I was linked to a guy called Pat (Patrick) O'Sullivan. Pat was a quiet man, stood 6'2" tall and who had a reputation of being able to look after himself. My only hope was that he could look after me too. It was an odd coupling as I was still quite small for my age and he a mountain of a man. We were soon nicknamed 'Little and Large'. This was well before the comedy duo 'Little and Large' had become known to the general public in the UK and quite possibly well before the comedy duo had actually first met. Pat and I were like chalk and cheese but immediately we became firm friends. Pat liked my outgoing attitude and I respected Pat's quiet approach to life. We ate together, slept next to one another and stayed close to one another when out on exercise. I learned so much from Pat in self-preservation and he in turn looked out for my wellbeing.

On the second day, we had to march deep into the rainforest carrying overnight equipment, food, guns, clean clothing, a sleeping bag, medical equipment and a bivouac. It was adventurous but very uncomfortable. This place was a typical tropical rainforest being hot, wet and very humid. The forest supported a wide range of different species that were to be avoided if at all possible. Snakes, some venomous, rats, spiders (again some venomous), biting insects, leaches and other creepy crawlies that had a habit of finding their way inside clothing. The forest floor is of a red/brownish colour because of the leaf mass and was spongy to walk on. The smell which is emitted within a rainforest is of rotting vegetation and not particularly pleasant.

Late into the afternoon, we were told that the enemy that we were looking for had been seen within this locality. We were told to keep quiet and 'keep our eyes peeled'. We trod carefully scanning the undergrowth and trying to peer forwards and backwards through the trees. There wasn't any sign of anything. We even looked for breaks to plant life which might have been caused by people passing or treading too heavily. Tension began to rise and any little noise made all of us jump, our hearts began to pound in our chests and breathing was hard to control. After about 30 minutes, we were signalled to keep low. Pat pushed me into some undergrowth, which I didn't appreciate but accepted that it was his job to do what was right. Pat indicated that I should keep quiet but to keep alert. He indicated that he was going to climb one of the trees to see if you could get a clearer picture of our surroundings and to also see if there was any movement from our invisible enemy. Pat began the climb disappearing in the lower branches of the tree. Everything remained quiet until the silence was disturbed with Pat's booming voice.

"You sneaky little fucking bastards. Wait till I get my fucking hands on you. You're all fucking dead meat. Let me fucking down."

I looked towards where the voice was coming from. To my amazement and only just in view, I saw two boots jutting through a branch of the tree Pat had climbed. Several other marines suddenly appeared from nowhere.

"Where's Pat?" they asked.

"He went up that tree," I replied. "I think those are his boots in that branch," I pointed upwards.

The marines scattered as quickly as they had arrived, most into the undergrowth and two went up the tree.

"Clear," called a voice and the marines appeared back to where I was hiding. I stood up and moved with the marines to the base of the tree. We looked up towards where the boots were hanging and saw Pat, stung up on a branch of the tree by his wrists. Ropes had been quickly and efficiently tied to the branch and Pat's wrists, yet there was no sign of the perpetrators. Whoever had done this to Pat had disappeared like 'will o' the wisp'. After releasing Pat and gathering all of the marines together, we returned to base camp. We learned later that several Ghurkhas had been sitting up the tree Pat had climbed and had been watching as we scanned the area. As Pat ascended the tree, the Ghurkhas had grabbed him, tied his wrists with rope, attached him to the branch of the tree and pushed him off the branch so that he could not get a safe grip or to manage getting back on the tree. The Ghurkhas had then moved through the trees until out of sight of their pursuers. It is understandable why the Japanese were fearful of the Ghurkhas during WWII as they were admirable adversaries. Silent, deadly, skilled Jungle fighters, the Ghurkhas were unafraid and passionate supporters of the British crown. In camp, we set up our bivouacs, cooked a meal from the ration packs we had been given and prepared to bed down for the night. Pat gave me a rope and told me to place the rope in a circle around my sleeping bag. He told me that the rope would deter snakes from crawling over us in the night. As it happened, it did not deter rats. During the night, I was awoken several times as rats moved to get close to me to keep warm. There is nothing more off putting than to have rats trying to snuggle up in your groin area and under your arms. The following day, we broke camp, packed everything away and was airlifted back to the ship.

When back in the mess, I took great pleasure telling my story of the previous three days with the marines and of what had happened to Pat.

Chapter Eight
Returning to Singapore

Being docked in Singapore was always a pleasure. Although noisy during the day on board ship, evenings were quiet apart from the sound of steam being pumped onto the ship to run auxiliary machinery. More engineering tasks had to be completed throughout our second stay, but life was more relaxed. Being in the boiler room allowed me time to learn more and even practice some of the tasks that the duty POME carried out. During this time in Singapore, we had Captain's rounds. This is where the Captain visited all departments on the ship and checked that everywhere was spick and span. Before the rounds, everything in the boiler room had to be cleaned to an immaculate level. In the boiler room, there were many brass gauges which had to be polished and the decks, handrails and other equipment had to be scrubbed. When the Captain came to do his rounds, everything within the boiler room gleamed. It was with pride that we were awarded a star rating.

When leaving the ship for shore leave, we always anticipated a good time. Every time we left the ship and walked towards the main gate of the dock yard, the heady smell of jasmine in the air always lifted our spirits and almost gave one the impression that everything was right in the world. Because the NAAFI in the dockyard was always a focal point for time off during the day, many happy hours were spent there swimming and relaxing. It was during this second stay in Singapore and at the NAFFI that I bumped into my old CPO from Raleigh Chief Giddings. It was so strange seeing him in a different guise. No longer was he training and instructing me but was taking over as CPO of the engine room on HMS Albion. Chief Giddings was now a colleague, and this transition I found quite difficult to deal with. CPO Giddings would always have my utmost respect but to be able to sit with him and drink together as mates, I found uncomfortable. CPO Giddings would often come over and sit with us ratings and have a drink with us, but I was always on my best behaviour. On several occasions, he joined us ratings on a run ashore to Singapore main town and to Bugis street but his presence always made me feel uncomfortable. It's silly, but I think that I was trying to protect him in some way. Perhaps I didn't want him to see any bad or silly behaviour, yet I'm sure he would have been like us when he was a rating.

One of the most annoying people on board the Albion was a guy called Clarkie. 'Clarkie' had not made many friends on board and tended to keep to himself. However, Clarkie, at every occasion when we docked, would stand by the 'Goffer' Machine (a machine that sold soft drinks) and would ask everyone who passed if they had ten pence to give him so that he could get a drink. His excuse was that he didn't have any change. As you can imagine, on a ship as large as the Albion and with over 1,500 people on board, Clarkie was given lots of ten pence pieces as individuals passed by. Later, you would see Clarkie enjoying a night out spending the ten pences he had collected. By the second time we were in Singapore, the guy's on board had become attuned to Clarkie's scam and money was not as forthcoming in the same way. Some of the guy's also resented the fact that Clarkie was 'ripping people off'. One evening whilst in Nisoon, a group of guy's saw Clarkie in a bar. He was totally inebriated and so much so, could hardly stand. Clarkie is one guy who would never join in with group activities whilst ashore and had insisted that he would never follow like sheep. Hence, Clarkie had never been to Bugis street, nor had he had a tattoo. Some of the guy's got together and planned to pull Clarkie into an activity that was opposite to what he would have agreed. The guy's decided to join Clarkie and encouraged him to drink more alcohol. After a few hours, Clarkie was well and truly 'out of it', virtually unconscious. At this point, the guy's carried Clarkie to 'Jonnie Ghurkhas' where he was placed on a tattooing bed, had his trousers and pants removed and was tattooed on his backside. Not having a design in mind, the guy's started with the suggestion that he should have elephants tattooed on each cheek of his backside, walking into the cheeks and disappearing. In total, seven elephants were imprinted for life, four on one side and three on the other. To add colour, a small pond was placed on one cheek with a boy sitting under a palm tree. The other cheek was finished off with a crocodile hiding in undergrowth and just above, the sun setting. All of which had been carefully fitted within the pant line of his underwear.

After taking Clarkie back to the ship and placing him on his bunk face down, he was left to recover. The next morning Clarkie woke with a hangover and you could see that he was uncomfortable. Clarkie kept touching his backside and you could see by his reaction that it was raw and sore. No one in the mess acknowledged Clarkie and deliberately did not make eye contact with him. Everyone in the mess knew what had happened the previous night and all were smiling, trying hard not to laugh out loud. Eventually Clarkie got out of his bunk and went for a shower. We all thought that on his return, Clarkie would be angry and out for revenge, but as it happened, nothing was said. Apparently, Clarkie didn't know about the tattoo for several days and when he found that he had the tattoos, kept very quiet. It also stopped him from asking for money from everyone.

After a week, we sailed again, this time only for a few days. The ship was destined to be involved in a night assault exercise. The exercise took place off the Marang area of the Malaysian coastline. In the company of a number of other warships and auxiliaries, war games took place. HMS Albion was centre to these activities, flying marines and Ghurkhas onto the mainland. Marang is located in the South China Sea and is a small coastal town located in the province of Terengganu, Malaysia. At the time, Marang, boasted only a small fishing community but had wonderful beaches. We were joined by ships from the US fleet, Australian and New Zealand Navy and army personnel. The exercise went well and on our return to Singapore, we were granted leave. Several of us decided that as a result of the exercise, we all wanted to visit Merang for some well-earned rest and relaxation.

We travelled from Singapore, across the causeway into Johor Bahru and boarded a bus. It took about ten hours to reach our destination, stopping at Hentian Bandar, Kuantan and then Merang. There was no accommodation available in Merang at that time apart from fishermen's lodges. We decided to make camp on the beach and tried to live Robinson Crusoe style. The locals looked on in amazement and thought it highly amusing that a small group of Westerners had moved into their domain. After living on the beach for two days, having little food available and having run out of beer, we packed up to return by bus. Although we were abysmally poor Robinson Crusoe's, we all enjoyed our experience. Swimming and sunbathing during the day, cooking on open fires, having night bonfires and just enjoying each other's company. If ever there was a paradise, this was the place. I often think that every young person should experience days like this, living out in the open, fending for themselves and enjoying the company of friends.

The bus journey both ways was rather eventful. We boarded with locals, were given snacks by those on the bus and shared some of the food that we had brought with us, including crisps, chocolate and salted nuts. The snacks offered us were non-commercial, and included food stuffs that I had never seen before or had ever tasted. It was difficult to establish exactly what was in these snacks but they tasted good. The locals laughed as we tried each item. I guess it was because we all tended to sniff the food, examine it before tasting and then trying the tiniest piece before devouring it. Some of the snacks we tried were dried insects. We only tried one or two but the locals devoured these like royalty eating caviar. We also tried to have conversations with the locals, but no one seemed to know any English. Our sign language was pretty pathetic too. We sat next to boxes containing chickens, ducks and the occasional pig. I'm not sure whether the livestock were charged to travel on the bus but it appeared that they were content and possibly had travelled this way many times. Life could not get better.

For the rest of our leave period, we decided to stay in Singapore City. Having booked a hotel, one we rarely used, we spent time getting to know the locals. The hotel was chosen because it was cheap and only had the very basic facilities. In our rooms, 'Chitchats' scurried up the walls and ceilings, consuming copious amounts of insects. The beds were hard but the bedding was clean and the pillow soft. We met a group of people on Changi beach and having spent the afternoon with them, were invited to join them for dinner at their homes. We ate, drank and laughed together, ending up staying for several days. People from Singapore are very hospitable or are not used to telling you that they have had enough and want you to leave. However, we made really good friends. The mix of people, Chinese, Malay and Indian provided interesting names. Most Singaporeans use Western names and were easy to remember. Malay, because of their links to Islam used Islamic names, like Abdul, Mohammed, Anil etc. whereas the Chinese maintained their cultural heritage names, such as Liu, Wang and Zhang. I made a particularly good friendship with Liu. Liu was the same age as me and he worked in his parents' restaurant. Liu's family were so hospitable and insisted in calling me their number two son. I learned so much about Chinese culture from Liu, he being keen to introduce me to the Chinese way of life. We attended festivals together, visited temples and I was introduced to all kinds of new food stuff. I became proficient in using chopsticks being tested by having to pick up individual grains of rice to much larger items of food.

Liu and I visited the Tiger Balm Gardens or Haw Par Villa as it is now called. Tiger Balm Gardens is the creation of Chinese-Burmese Aw Boon Haw and his brother Aw Boon Par, who, after amassing a fortune from their herbalist father's creation of Tiger Balm, built an art deco villa, and filled the gardens with models, statues and dioramas relating to their Chinese heritage and Buddhist beliefs. Tiger Balm is South East Asia's cure-all medical cream. During the 1970s Tiger Balm still contained opium and was not allowed to be sold in the UK. However, in Singapore and the rest of South East Asia, Tiger Balm was the one thing that everyone had in their medical kits. For us navy guy's, we used Tiger Balm regularly as a cure for hangovers. Just a little of this miraculous balm placed on each temple would almost instantaneously get rid of the headaches that accompanied handovers. In the Tiger Balm Gardens, there were thousands of models of different sizes. The gardens were dotted on a low hill overlooking the Singapore Strait, offering an eclectic mix of Chinese history, moral messages and an amazing scenic backdrop – all thanks to the massive wealth accrued from Tiger Balm. Some of the models also contain Tiger Balm products, suggesting the park was also an early form of product placement and guerrilla marketing.

Liu and I also visited Bugis Street on a regular basis meeting Big Angie who still called me her 'Cherry Boy'. For some reason, I always felt safer in Bugis Street with Liu, as he knew many of the people who worked there. The hustle and bustle of Bugis Street during the 1970s is hard to describe, but having visited recently, Bugis Street has lost much of its magic. It is still a wonderful place to visit with its new shopping mall and street seating area but it does feel sterile. The transvestites of Bugis Street began to rendezvous in this area during the 1950s, they attracted increasing numbers of Western tourists who came for the booze, the food, the 'pasar malam' shopping (market) and the "girls". Business boomed during the early part of the 1970s and Bugis Street became a lively and bustling area, forming the heart of *Xiao Po*. It was one of Singapore's most famous tourist attractions from the 1950s to the 1980s, renowned internationally for its nightly parade of flamboyantly dressed transvestites and it attracted hordes of Caucasian gawkers who had never before witnessed Asian queens in full regalia. The Kaytai's would tease, cajole visitors, sit on visitors' laps or pose for photographs for a fee. Others would sashay up and down the street looking to hook half-drunk sailors, American GI's, and other foreigners for an hour of profitable intimacy. Not only would these clients get the thrill of sex with an exotic oriental, there would be the added spice of transgressing gender boundaries in a steamy hovel. There was an adage amongst Westerners that one could easily tell who was a real female and who was not: The Kaytai's were drop-dead gorgeous, while the rest who were real women were very plain and tended to wear practical clothing. The amount of revenue that the transvestites of Bugis Street raked in was considerable, providing a booster shot in the arm for the tourism industry. The street was popularly called *'Boogie Street'* by British servicemen. Veterans recall that the notorious drinking section began from Victoria Street West to Queen Street. Halfway between Victoria and Queen Streets, there was an intersecting lane parallel to the main roads, also lined with *al fresco* bars. There was a well-patronised public toilet with a flat roof of which there are archival photos, complete with jubilant rooftop transvestites. One of the 'hallowed traditions' bestowed upon the area by sojourning sailors (usually from Britain, Australia, and New Zealand), was the ritualistic 'dance of the flaming arseholes' on top of the toilet's roof. Compatriots on the ground would chant the signature tune "Haul 'em down you Zulu warrior" sung whilst the sailors performed their act. They would sing, dance, drink then flash their backsides to all and sundry. Over the years this became almost a mandatory exercise and although it may seem too many to be a gross act of indecency, it was generally well received by the sometimes up to hundreds of tourists and locals. The Kaytai's or Beanie Boys, as the transvestites were referred to by Anglophile white visitors, certainly did not mind either. By the mid-1970s however, Singapore started a crackdown on this type of lewd behaviour and sailors were arrested at gunpoint by the local authorities for upholding the tradition. By this time those sailors brave enough to try it were dealt with severely and even shipped home in disgrace. Though many locals accepted this part of Singaporean culture, many conservative Singaporeans felt that it was a disgrace and it defaced Singapore's image.

After just a few short weeks, HMS Albion was ready to sail again, which meant I had to say a fond farewell to Liu and his family but an invitation was given for me to return to their family home on our return to Singapore.

Chapter Nine
Australia

Singapore to Fremantle was a rough passage. We left Singapore heading towards Jakarta, then into the Indian Ocean to arrive in Fremantle on 9 August 1971 for an eight-day visit. We had to shift from our tropical uniform (whites) to blue uniform (blues) for the Australian winter. It is 2686 nautical miles from Singapore to Fremantle Australia and the climate change is notable, particularly in the Australian winter.

We were so much looking forward to visiting Australia having heard of the warm welcome many of the guys had had when they had previously visited Sidney. However, Fremantle is so very different to Sydney, not only geographically, but also culturally. Monday is never a good day to dock in a new country as the weekend had finished and normal working days often commenced on Mondays. Fremantle is a port city in Western Australia, located at the mouth of the Swan River in the metropolitan area of Perth, the state capital. Fremantle Harbour serves as the port of Perth. It is about ten miles from Fremantle to Perth and public transport was fairly good. Fremantle played a key role in WWII as the largest submarine base in the Southern Hemisphere. Post-war immigration from Europe, particularly Italy, helped shape Fremantle's character. Fremantle is recognised for its well-preserved Victorian and Edwardian streetscapes and convict-era heritage, and is known as a bohemian enclave with a thriving arts and culinary scene. It is also the traditional home of the Fremantle Football Club one of two Australian Football League teams based in Western Australia.

The first Europeans to visit modern-day Fremantle were Dutch explorers who mapped the area and went up the Swan River, it was reported by the Dutch explorers that this place would be an ideal place for a settlement however; no attempts were made by the Dutch to start such settlements here. It wasn't until 1872 when Captain James Stirling aboard HMS Success explored the coastline near to the Swan River that any consideration was made to develop a British settlement. As a result of Stirling's report to the British Government, Captain Charles Fremantle of HMS Challenger, a 603-ton, 28-gun frigate, was instructed to sail to the west coast of Australia to establish a settlement there. On 2 May 1829, Fremantle hoisted the Union Flag in a bay near to what is now known as Arthur Head, and in accordance with his instructions, took formal possession of the whole of the West Coast of what was then called New Holland in the name of Britain's King George IV. The settlement of Perth began on 12 August 1829. Captain Fremantle left the colony on 25 August after providing much assistance to Stirling in setting up the colony. It was then that Stirling decided to name the port settlement 'Fremantle'. In early September 1829, the merchant vessel *Anglesea* grounded at Gage Roads, at the mouth of the Swan River. She did not break up, as had been expected, but instead survived to become Western Australia's first prison hulk. On 1 June 1850, the first convicts arrived at Fremantle aboard the Scindian. The thirty-seventh and last convict ship to dock at Fremantle was the Houhoumont on 10 January 1868, signalling the end of penal transportation to Australia. Among the 280 convicts on board were 62 Fenian military and political prisoners – members of the Irish Republican Brotherhood – six of whom managed to escape the Convict Establishment in the Catalpa rescue of 1876. During this period, notorious South Sea pirate, Bully Haynes lived in Fremantle with his fiancée Miss Scott, daughter of the Fremantle Harbour Master.

In the early years of European settlement, the port comprised various wooden jetties in the area known as Bathers Beach and Arthur Head. These jetties were exposed to the elements, including the strong south-westerly winds known locally as the Fremantle Doctor. Work began on the Fremantle Inner Harbour, designed by State Engineer CY O'Connor, in 1892 and the harbour was officially opened on 4 May 1897.

Since then, the port has played a significant part in Western Australia's development and history, including wartime. Deepwater bulk facilities in the Outer Harbour, 22 kilometres south at Kwinana, were first developed in 1955 to service the Kwinana industrial area, which expanded rapidly in the 1960s and '70s. This expansion was still taking place when we docked. The feeling one got when in Fremantle and Perth during 1971 was of an old pre-war Britain. Many of the people there still followed old British tradition, especially around the drinking of alcohol. All bars and pubs closed at 10:00 pm on week days and

Saturdays and was not allowed to sell alcohol on Sundays. It seemed as if the whole of Fremantle and Perth went to church on Sundays as everyone would be dressed in their Sunday best. Women all wore hats and gloves and the men all in suits.

Perth did have a couple of night clubs La Riviera, Whisky-a-go-go and the Charles Hotel. I recall going to these venues to see 'Pieces of Eight', a successful duo that was big on the scene in Perth. The duo played at some of Perth's major night entertainment venues of that time. The act often performed in two or three separate venues in the one night, so as we moved from one venue to another, 'Pieces of Eight' followed. Their floorshow was heavily geared towards performances made famous by the Everly Brothers and Simon and Garfunkel. It felt to us matelot's a little 'Old Hat' but the locals seemed to enjoy it, especially when there was audience participation. The whole experience seemed rather conservative too. Our ship's company had been introduced to the wilder side of entertainment, particularly in Singapore, so to see people of our age group getting excited because someone had been kissed in full view of everyone else, we found this to be rather tame. Although I could brag that I had been to Australia, the visit was rather disappointing in many respects.

After a week in Fremantle, it was good to be back at sea again, especially knowing that we were going back to Singapore. We were due to dock in Singapore and spend another month there. Going back to Singapore was like going home. I was looking forward just to be back in my spiritual home but was also happy because I would be seeing Liu and his family again. There was a real sense of excitement aboard and the journey couldn't go fast enough. As it is approximately 2680 nautical miles from Fremantle to Singapore and if travelling at ten knots, would take eleven days. Our journey back to Singapore through the Indian Ocean and South China seas moved at snail's pace through inclement weather back to tropical weather. We changed from 'blues' back into our 'whites' and it felt good to be back in shorts. Along the way, we undertook sea trials, testing out the full capacity of Albion's engines and boilers. Being in the boiler room was hard work but exciting, especially when having to respond to the demands made on us to react to change in speed. The noise and temperature within the boiler room was at times excessive. To ensure that we did not damage our hearing, we had to wear ear protectors. Having to wear these became uncomfortable when the temperature increased. The sweat accumulated around the plastic seal and the moisture would collect around the ear. This meant that we continuously had to remove the ear protectors to wipe the protectors and our ears. Had we not done this, you quite quickly would begin to have sweat rashes that were quite painful. We also had to keep hydrated and so there was an endless flow of orange and lemon drinks on offer. These drinks were made using a powder mixed with water and then adding ice to ensure that the liquid was drinkable. I was never sure whether these drinks had been contaminated with oil or whether the natural oils from the citrus powder actually tainted the flavour. Because of the need to drink copious amounts of cold liquids, trips to the ice maker were regular. It was not easy humping large blocks of ice from where the ice maker's shop was to the boiler room, particularly because trying to get these blocks through the airlock and down several flights of steep ladders was akin to doing an assault course. We were also ordered to take salt tablets when working in the boiler room and when temperatures were excessive. These tablets were huge and had to be swallowed whole. Equivalent to the size of a ten pence piece, these tablets were even difficult just to fit in the mouth. Those of us in the boiler room would bet on how long it would take to swallow these tablets and would laugh as each in turn gagged as the salt tablets got lodged on the way down our throats.

Life felt so good on board ship. We had no televisions but did have the ships radio station, manned by volunteers who would become DJs in their spare time. I became a regular presenter on 'Radio Albion'. The radio station was located in a very small compartment, just big enough to allow two people to move around. We were well stocked with records and my particular genre of music was Motown, Soul and the occasional Blues' song thrown in for good measure. My signature tune was Thunder Clap Newman's *Something in the Air*. I felt particularly lucky to be part of the ships radio station and would always have numerous requests. Aretha Franklin's *Spanish Harlem*; Marvin Gaye's *Mercy Mercy Me* and *What's Going On* were prime favourites as well as Al Greens *Tired Of Being Alone*; Isaac Hayes theme From *Shaft*; Michael Jackson's *Got To Be There*; The Jackson Five *Never Can Say Goodbye*; Carole King's double A side single *It's Too Late/I Feel The Earth Move*; The Supremes *Nathan Jones*; Ike and Tina Turner's *Proud Mary*; Bill Withers *Ain't No Sunshine* and my particular favourite, Stevie Wonder's *If You Really Love Me* among hundreds of others. The ship also had a large BBC Radio collection of comedies; 'Round the Horne'; 'The Navy Lark'; 'Benny Hill Time' and 'The Clitheroe Kid' being firm favourites.

During the evenings at sea, film projectors were also set up in the galley mess after dinner. Each evening we were presented with a main feature film. James Bond in *Diamonds Are Forever; A Clock Work Orange; Shaft and The Andromeda Strain* are a few I can recall. The highlight however was the Tom and Jerry cartoons. Remembering how hundreds of sailors would pack themselves into the galley mess just to see the cartoons still fills me with a real sense of joy. When the credits came on, everyone would shout 'Good Old Fred' as Fred Quimby's name came on screen. Fred Quimby was the producer of many of the Tom and Jerry's cartoons. Everyone would cheer, stamp their feet and whistle as the cartoon began, then utter silence as the cartoon progressed, interspersed with rigorous bouts of laughter as Tom was smashed, beaten up, or received an injury. Great cheers arose when Jerry escaped Tom's pursuit and evaded Tom's plans, then at the end clapping and cheers from everyone. Copious amounts of beer were drunk during these sessions and tons of chocolate consumed. These evenings always seemed to be better when 'Baby's Heads' (individual steak and kidney pudding) and 'Shit on a raft' (sautéed kidneys served on toast) had been on the menu for dinner. Just a quick note, to ensure that the sautéed kidneys didn't run off the toast, the chefs would pipe a wall of mashed potatoes around the edge of the toast making a nest for the kidneys to rest in.

We had the occasional Al Fresco on the flight deck on our journey back to Singapore. The reason for these 'party' type events was to maintain morale. Al Fresco's on board ship were momentous occasions as the preparation for these events took considerable planning and were a logistical nightmare. Barbeques had to be set up in an area that was free of any danger, away from aviation fuel lines and machinery; tables had to be brought up from lower decks to serve the food being cooked; food and drink had to be transported from the galley as well as all of the cooking equipment, including servers, cutlery, plates etc., and containers to take away waste products and dirty items. Firefighting equipment had to be strategically placed, just in case something did go wrong and a Public Address system brought up from the radio station along with records for incidental music to be played. Feeding such a large number of ratings who were always hungry must have scared the chefs to death, however, the chefs on board always rose to any occasion and produced some excellent spreads. Out in the open ocean, there is a strange feeling of togetherness on board a ship but also a sense of isolation. Imagine, nothing around you for possibly thousands of miles only the occasional sea bird and dolphin to keep you company, yet having the hustle and bustle of 1600 ships company enjoying time together. At these Al Fresco's, there was always some form of entertainment, from raucous singing of songs like *Wild Rover*, *Mary of the Mountain Glen* and dirty rugby songs, to mini Olympic games such as 'Tug Of War', 'Five a side football', 'Deck running', 'Volley Ball', 'Obstacle Racing'; 'Medicine Ball Throwing' and such like. Games such as cricket and baseball were never played as too many balls would have been lost at sea. Never far from mind though was of us returning back to Singapore.

Chapter Ten
Home from Home

As we docked in Singapore ratings were immediately kept busy getting the ship ready for our next voyage, restocking the ship, re-fuelling, carrying out general maintenance, painting and fulfilling our everyday duties. We had a month to look forward to in Singapore, but how quickly that month evaporated into time.

Going ashore again was like being at home. On leaving the dockyard, people from Sembawang village greeted us as if we were family who had arrived to stay with them for a while. It felt as if we knew everyone in Sembawang, from the bar tenders and girls who worked within the bars, to the shop keepers, food stall holders, women from the brothel, dockyard workers and those employed at the NAAFI. We met up with old naval friends, some who had been on board Albion but who we had not seen whilst in Australia or at sea. It's funny, but being on such a large vessel like Albion and because there were so many people living on board, it occasionally happened that people would not meet until back of terra firma. I remember hearing of brothers who had served on HMS Ark Royal (the largest of the Royal Navy carriers at that time), which had a ship's company of 2,250 (2,640 inc. air staff) and which was 36,800 tons (as built) 43,060 tons 53,950 tons full and was 804 ft long, who never met on board and had both served at the same time for well over a year. When we met old friends, it was if we had never been apart. We started where we left off and exchanged many stories of our adventures, where we had been, what we had been doing and what we did that shouldn't or couldn't be repeated. We also met up with other matelot's from other British Naval Ships who were also in Singapore at that time and who had on occasion had accompanied HMS Albion as escorts. All carriers had to have at least one or two smaller vessels accompanying them on their voyages. These other vessels, often Frigates or Destroyers were there to ensure that the larger carriers were not attacked by enemy forces. Submarines were also used to protect carriers too, frequently not seen by even the British surface vessels but always monitoring the unseen enemy hidden below the surface of the oceans and seas we travelled.

We also met up with friends and families from other parts of Singapore who we had become acquainted with. I met up with Liu and his family and was happy when they invited me to stay with them when I was able. Liu and I were like brothers. Strange as it may sound, I think because we were of the same age, the bond which we made felt somehow stronger than the bond I had for my birth siblings. At home, I had four brothers, but the age difference between us all was quite big, my eldest brother being 21 years older than me and the brother closest in age was six years older. Liu and I had more in common than I had had with my brothers. We shared the same interests, the same past time activities, the same taste in music and just loved being together. Liu shared his bedroom with me and had even made space for me to hang clothing and a place to keep personal items. We almost never disagreed, would compromise and were always accepting of one another's point of view. Living with Liu's family was also like living with my own family. They never made demands upon me, yet expected me to help with cooking, cleaning and taking part in family activities. I could move around the house as I wanted, help myself to drinks and food when I wanted, to go to bed and get up when it pleased me and even to come 'home' whenever I wanted. Liu's parents even gave me my own key to the house. Liu would also come to meet me at Sembawang after I finished my duties and we frequently had a few beers in the Melbourne Bar, the Avondale or in the Ocean Bar. Liu was also good friends with some of the traders in Sembawang and as a result, if I wanted to buy anything, I would always get a discount.

Singapore is blessed with having wonderful and consistent warm weather all year round. Yes, humidity is high but strangely enjoyable. When it rains in Singapore, it does so with vengeance. There were days when the rain fell so heavily that it was difficult to see where you were going. These heavy down pours didn't last long but enough water filled the monsoon ditched that paralleled many of the roads. The speed of water that gushed down the monsoon ditches was sufficient to clear them of debris and wild life and had the added advantage of cleaning them out. After the rain, came the sunshine. Roads, pathways and puddles soon dried up increasing the humidity. I remember standing watching the roads as soon as the rain had stopped and watching in wonderment at the speed the water evaporated. The intensity of the sun on the wet surface caused steam to form, like low level fog. It was only after these torrential downpours that the humidity became a problem. Having a change of underwear was always an advantage.

Like the weather, things in Singapore were beginning to change dramatically too, particularly around the dockyard. This was because in 1967, the British had announced their plans to withdraw their troops from Singapore, to the dismay of the Singapore government. Initially, the deadline had been set for the mid-1970s but this plan was brought forward to 1971. The sudden pull-out of British forces presented serious problems to Singapore's defence and economic security because at the time, the Singapore Armed Forces was in its infancy, and the British military bases were contributing over 20 percent to Singapore's gross national product. To counter these problems, Singapore embarked on a rapid industrialisation programme, tightened its labour laws to attract foreign investments, strengthened its defence through military cooperation with other countries, and tripled its military spending. By the deadline, Singapore had achieved strong economic growth and nearly full employment.

It was at this time that Liu announced that he was joining the Singapore armed force and had signed up to join their army. In many ways, I was pleased for Liu and proud of his decision but recognised that he was preparing me for his imminent departure. Before the month was through, Liu left to take up his post in basic training. It was a heart-breaking time tinged with pride. We both knew that this would be our final farewell and the chances of meeting again would be remote. Our final night was spent having dinner with his family and reminiscing about the days we had spent together. After Liu had departed, I spent more time in Sembawang, rarely visiting Singapore city. The last two weeks were a busy time on board. We were due to sail again on 20 September and would be returning to Singapore for one last time. On our return, we would be heading the withdrawal of British troops from Singapore and officially handing over the Dockyard to the Singapore authorities. This early preparation was to ensure that everything would be ready for the final withdrawal and in preparation for our long voyage home. When it became clear that Britain's decision to withdraw was irreversible, Singapore leaders quickly began to plan for their future. They successfully negotiated with the British for a soft loan of £50 million, free transfer of key assets, help with operating the air-defence system, and training of their military staff. In the same year, the Bases Economic Conversion Department was set up to oversee the conversion and commercialisation of lands and facilities, including the naval bases that had belonged to the British. These assets were to be instrumental in propelling Singapore's shipbuilding industry forward.

There was a real sense of urgency amongst the ship's company and many of the guys needed to say their goodbyes to friends they had made. One of the guys in particular was having a really difficult time. He had fallen in love with a Malaysian girl called Gina. He and Gina were inseparable and they decided to marry. This meant that permission had to be granted by the captain and something needed to be sorted so that he could spend time with Gina, after all, he would not be allowed to bring Gina with him. A group of his closest friends decided to try to offer support by researching what possibilities were available to him so that he would not be parted from Gina. He clearly could not remain in Singapore because of the British withdrawal and it appeared that Gina would not be able to go to the UK with him. Our problem solving sessions provided him with a lifeline. He would request a transfer to the Australian forces who were remaining in Singapore for the foreseeable future; then he would be able to marry Gina at his leisure and thereafter could make arrangements for Gina to join him in the UK on his return. As things turned out, he was given a transfer to the Australian forces, did marry Gina, but eventually settled in Sidney Australia following his discharge from the Royal Australian Navy. I heard much later that they ended up as a large family with Gina giving birth to seven children.

We busied ourselves with the preparation for sailing and for the imminent withdrawal. Machinery that was not wanted or needed anymore had to be off loaded onto the dockyard and items of importance that were stored within the dockyard had to be loaded onto the Albion to be returned to England. After all, the Albion was the largest British vessel in Singapore docks and the only ship to have the capacity to return these items to the UK. Not everything was completed at this time, but the preparation enabled the ship to collect all essential items after a further tour and return to Singapore.

During this month in Singapore, I also met up with CPO Giddings again. CPO Giddings had taken an interest in my progression and began preparing me for advancement to Killick. I knew that it would be some time before I would get a promotion but CPO Giddings told me of the things I needed to know and do in order for such a promotion to happen. On a couple of occasions, CPO Giddings and I went to Kusu Island, where there were unexplored beaches. During one of these visits, we found a beach near to a mangrove. Sitting on the beach we suddenly saw Mud Skippers (Gobiidae). Mud Skippers are particularly abundant in mangroves and muddy shores, but some, like the Golden Spotted Mud Skippers are also commonly seen on rocky shores and near reefs. It was fascinating to see these small fish walking along the wet sand, stopping occasionally to shake their heads to re-oxygenate the water they held in their mouths so that they could breathe. We were also lucky to see Pied Oriental hornbills which had nested close to the beach. These last few days were to become fixed in my mind and in many ways helped me to prepare for leaving this wonderful place. Once the month was over, we set sail again, steaming towards the Philippines.

Chapter Eleven
Subic Bay

Steaming through the South China Sea, we covered the 1608 nautical miles to Subic Bay in the Philippines. We were at sea for just over a week arriving at the US Naval Base, Subic Bay. Subic Bay was a major ship-repair, supply, and rest and recreation facility, once under the custodianship of the Spanish, then under British rule and subsequently taken over by the United States Navy. Located in Zambales province, Philippines, the base was some 262 square miles, about the size of Singapore. The US Navy base boasted the largest volume of sales of any exchange in the world at Subic Bay, and the Naval Supply Depot handled the largest volume of fuel oil of any navy facility in the world. The naval base was the largest overseas naval installation of the United States Armed Forces.

During the Vietnam War, Subic Bay was at the peak of its activities and home to the US Seventh Fleet. The average number of ships visiting the Subic Bay during this period increased dramatically from an average of 98 in 1964 to its highest number of 215 by 1967. When we arrived in Subic Bay, the number of ships visiting the base had reduced but numbers remained high. The base had six wharves, two piers, and 160 mooring points and anchorages and the main 'Alava' pier was over 600 feet long. In 1967, over 4,224,503 sailors visited Subic Bay in support of the war in Vietnam. It is said that these sailors spent more than $25 million in duty-free goods from the Navy Exchange whilst there and spent a considerable amount more in the adjoining city of Olongapo.

Subic Bay was a microcosm of the United States in that everything available within the US appeared to be available here. McDonalds, Kentucky Fried Chicken and other major food outlets all had diners located within the base. Cinemas, bowling allies, ice rinks, sports grounds, gyms and other recreational places were available to the multitude of service personnel working or visiting the base. The only people who could not access these facilities were the Filipinos

113

who were employed there. I guess all of the guys from HMS Albion were awestruck by the size of this base and of all the conveniences on offer to their American counterparts. However, although all of these amenities were on offer to us Brits, many of us declined the opportunity open to us, preferring to explore the true taste of the Philippines.

From the main gate leading out of Subic Bay stood a bride over the Olongapo River. The river was known to the Americans as 'shit' river and led to the beginning of Magsaysay Drive in Olongapo City. The river itself was an estuary, not holding copious amounts of water but was a bed full of thick smelly silt and mud. As you crossed the bridge, we saw many American service personnel throwing coins over the hand rail to fall into the quagmire below. Seated on thin wooden boats in the river were dozens of young children (the children's ages spanning anything from five years old to about 12 years old). As the coins landed in the thick dense mud of the river bed, the children would dive into this pit of horror to try to retrieve and collect as much money as they could get their hands on. The scene was quite shocking to us Brits and many of us did not find this activity amusing. We heard that on occasion, children had actually disappeared in the mud and had never been recovered. The blatant disrespect for life, especially children's lives was abhorrent to us visitors but to the many Americans, this was seen as just a way of life.

Many of the US service men going into Olongapo were marines, many of them doing tours in Vietnam. Being as it is only 716 nautical miles from Subic Bay to Vietnam, many had been on several tours there. It is without doubt that many of these marines and naval personal had been involved directly in combat situations and some had a distinct vacant look in their eyes. It is quite possible that many also suffered from post-traumatic stress, so their behaviour in throwing coins over the bridge into the mud of the Olongapo River for the children to collect had not registered as being a dangerous activity. What was noticeable was that most of the marines were not much older than me, yet had gone through so much.

The many bars and nightclubs along Ramon Magsaysay Drive between the naval base main gate and Rizal Avenue were notoriously popular. As you can imagine, having over four million service personnel visiting Subic Bay each year was for the locals and service personnel alike, a real focal point. To describe Olongapo's main streets is difficult, as we had torrential rain while we were there and so streets were often flooded to a point where we almost swam our way up the various streets. Luckily, bright coloured taxis (Jeepneys) were on hand and a short ride did not cost the earth. Jeepneys, which are sometimes just called jeeps, are Filipino buses and the most popular means of public transportation. Jeepneys are everywhere in the Philippines and are known for their crowded seating and outlandish decorations. Jeepneys have become a widespread symbol of Philippine culture and art, always painted in very bright colours and having religious trinkets hung around their peripheries.

In each of the bars were musicians and singers. The Filipinos are particularly good singer and many of them could hold an audience for hours, or until they were to drunk or spaced out to listen. Drugs were on sale everywhere. When I say drugs, I mean Cannabis and Marijuana and LSD (Lysergic acid diethylamide or Acid) as these were the most popular and most available illicit drugs at the time. Some people had access to opiates too, but by and large the former drugs were used most frequently by the Americans. Of course there was a never ending flow of cheap San Miguel beer for sale, lots of cheap spirits (none of which actually tasted anything like what they had on the label) and an assortment of cocktails, all with sexualised names and many referring to female genitalia. Central in all bars and hanging from the ceiling were film projectors. These projectors looped pornographic films that were shown on the four walls of each of the bars. These films were hard core porn many of which were American or locally made. There were lots of teenage prostitutes both in and outside of the bars, some as young 12 years old and the oldest around 20 years old. Some of the prostitutes also starred in the films being projected. Sex floor shows complemented the films on show taking place on demand and at a small cost to those requesting it. The debauchery was crushing and I can imagine that after visiting these bars several times, even the most hardened veteran would become bored. The majority of American vets were so out of their faces that the goings on around them blended in like trees to a forest.

Even when riding in the 'Jeepneys', the pressure from the drivers to get service personnel to part with their money was never-ending. The drivers would not only offer to take you to your chosen destination, but would also try to get you to buy watches, jewellery, pornographic literature, their wives, daughters, mothers, grandmothers, their sons or even themselves, drugs, food or any other contraband you could think of.

On one occasion whilst travelling in a 'Jeepney', the driver stopped at the side of a small pool, the pool, no bigger than an average residential garden in the

UK was watched and tended by a solitary figure. The Jeepney driver urged us out of the Jeepney and to follow him. Having followed the driver, he took us to the person sitting at the pool. Next to him were wooded crates filled with baby ducklings. We were encouraged to purchase a duckling, then to place this little ball of fluff onto the pool surface. Within seconds, there was a loud splash as a crocodile emerged from the dark water devouring the poor duckling in one gulp. We British sailors and animal lovers couldn't be done with this, so decided to buy as many ducklings as we could and save them from annihilation. We stuffed ducks in our jackets, under our hats and anywhere there was space. Word got out to other British sailors and they too began visiting the pond purchasing as many ducklings as they could hold. The Great British duckling rescue went into full swing. *Now there was a full size evacuation of ducklings in progress, but where to keep them?* Some of the ducklings were given to children we met as we walked along the streets. The children often having amazed looks on their faces, American service men might give then spare coins or even chocolate, but never ducklings. Some we released into the wild. Not the best thing I know, as these were farm reared ducklings and not very equipped to handle the dangers of the wild, and some would be taken on board to be kept as pets (not a good idea, pets are strictly not allowed). Having said this, I do have to confess that I did have a small 'chitchat' (lizard) that I had obtained in Singapore and which was tied by string to its rear leg and to my bunk. The 'chitchat' had lots of room to manoeuvre and was well fed. 'George' named after the late king, was an effective insect repellent, (not actually a repellent, but an eater of insects) keeping my bunk space clear of any unwanted flying insects. Ducklings were being smuggled on board HMS Albion at an alarming rate and were given special accommodation. Many were placed in buckets filled with fresh water and fed on bread, biscuits and cake and hidden in lockers; others were stowed away in machinery workshops, behind the ships guns and even in the stores. I recall seeing one of the Chinese chefs running out of the galley chasing a duckling with his machete, screaming at the top of his voice something that I can only presume to be foul language (sorry about the pun) but as I do not speak Cantonese, I can only assume that he was swearing. Executive orders came the following day that **ALL** ducklings had to be removed from the ship forthwith and that anyone not complying would be severely reprimanded. A crate had been set up on the dockyard for the duckling collection and was filled double quick time. It was heart-breaking to see such well-disciplined and strong young men cry as they parted with their 'babies', but I suppose it had to be done.

Whilst in Subic Bay there was a lot of hustle and bustle going on between the American, Australian, New Zealand and British top brass. Chauffer driven cars were transferring between ships and the main base offices. There was also a buss going around the ship as the Marines and Ghurkhas seemed to be preparing for something major. Speculation had it that we were possibly going to support the seventh fleet or the Australians and New Zealanders. We were aware that Britain was not involved with the action taking place in Vietnam but that didn't stop us from thinking policy might have changed back in the UK. In fact, policy had not changed in the UK and Britain was not joining their allies, well not under the British flag at least. This didn't stop the allied forces from recruiting a small contingent of marines, Ghurkhas and naval personnel to carry out activities as part of the Australian and New Zealand forces.

After leaving Subic Bay we steamed very close to Vietnam and actions began to take place. Marines and Ghurkhas were flown off the ship and I can only surmise that they were either taken into Vietnam or Cambodia. Some of us naval personnel were also involved in taking landing craft and fast boats towards the coast line dropping off and picking up our troops. Whether or not we were in Vietnam is debatable but would clearly be denied by the British government. However, we did spend sometime around the Vietnam coastal area and particularly around the Mekong Delta. The Mekong Delta located in southern Vietnam is a vast maze of rivers, swamps and islands. It was around this time that the Vietcong clashed with the Southern Vietnam forces and her allies escalating activities which ultimately resulted with the US withdrawal from Vietnam and the Communist North Vietnam taking control of capitalist South Vietnam. After several days of hurried activity in this area, we then steamed to Hong Kong, docking on 30 September, where Albion was alongside the British naval base, HMS Tamar.

Chapter Twelve
Hong Kong

On reaching Hong Kong, we were told that we would be remaining in Hong Kong for two-weeks. HMS Tamar had a fairly new dockyard being completed in 1962. The 'new' Tamar was compact following its reconstruction from the 'old Tamar' and HMS Albion appeared monstrous as it lay in its moorings. Because of the ongoing 'Cold War' the British had kept her navy presence in the Far East at high priority and even more modernisation plans were being drawn up to enhance Tamar's headquarter building. We were located in the Victoria area of Hong Kong but soon became more acquainted with Downtown Hong Kong (Main Island), Kowloon, Wan Chai and the New Territories. Hong Kong bay was a very busy waterfront housing many old style Chinese Junks, house boats as well as super large tankers. Traffic within the bay was so busy that one wonders how there wasn't daily collisions and the sinking of boats and ships. Also in the bay were long rowing type vessels; these housed all sorts of goods for sale to the locals who lived in the bay and also to visitors. Food stuff (mainly fruit, vegetables and fish) were being sold, as well as hot food, particularly noodle based dishes and kebabs. Ashore, Hong Kong was like no other place on earth. There were so many buildings and people crammed into such a small area, traffic was heavy and trying to mind map the area was virtually impossible.

I was excited to be in Hong Kong as my brother had been based in Hong Kong during his National Service during the late 1950s and, who I believe served with 36 Engineer Regiment based in Shek Knog and Sha Tin in the New Territories. I was excited to locate where my brother had been based and to see for myself the conditions he had described to me through his many stories of this area. I was also keen to locate the area where 'Virgin Soldiers' had been filmed in 1969. This had been one of my favourite films and had provided me with insight into National Service forces serving in Hong Kong during the 1950s.

Hong Kong typically distributed goods following the irregular coastline and transportation routes. The principal urban areas are established on Hong Kong Island and on the Kowloon Peninsula, where roughly half of the total population lives. Most of the population are concentrated around Victoria Harbour, living on the limited flatland that was starting to expand due to the authorities extending by reclaiming areas from the sea. Many major streets, especially those on the northern shore of Hong Kong Island, and much of the southern tip of the Kowloon Peninsula, have been built on reclaimed land.

Victoria Harbour is well protected because it is surrounded by mountains; Victoria Peak in the west, and Mount Parker in the east. Partly capped volcanic rocks and steep scar pike concaves lead to the inner harbour. Hong Kong Island and its islets have an area of only about 31 square miles, while urban Kowloon Island measure about 18 square miles. The New Territories account for the rest of the area, which is more than 90 percent of the total. The Victoria urban district located on the barren rocks of the north western coast of Hong Kong Island is the place where the British first landed in 1841, and it has since been the centre of administration and economy.

True to its original character as a fishing port, Hong Kong had a sizable, though rapidly dwindling marine settlement. The 'boat people', or Tanka as they are locally known, are essentially fisher folk living on junks and boats, as their ancestors did for centuries before them. They inhabit fishing towns, such as Aberdeen, Shau Kei Wan, and Cheung Chau areas. With the development of the urban areas and the decline of fishing activity, many of the Tanka worked ashore.

Nightlife in Downtown Hong Kong was always busy and buzzing. Shops never appeared to close, food was being cooked in every nook and cranny and the bars were 24/7. It's often said that New York never sleeps but Hong Kong must suffer from perpetual insomnia. Nights out in Hong Kong often started at the Royal China Fleet Club (the Seaman's mission). For those who managed to stay sober enough to continue their evening's activity, many would first go to Lan Kwai Fong on Hong Kong Island. The Lan Kwai Fong area was renowned for its amazing restaurants, bars and clubs. Another area, Soho, also had a wonderful feel to it but did not provide the unique Chinese experience as Lan Kwai Fong for those who were of a little more adventurous nature, the ferry to Kowloon was always a good option. Knutsford Terrance was the favourite hanging out place. Knutsford Terrance has a vibe of its own. This place had the all-night atmosphere of Lan Kwai Fong, was a little dirtier (the roads were just dirt tracks) but did not have the sleaze associated with Wan Chai. Some of the hardened veterans and most of the new comers to Hong Kong nearly always found themselves in Wan Chai. Wan Chai, on the northern shore of Hong Kong Island, has long been synonymous with 'yum-yum' prostitutes and vice. Wan Chai became legendary for its exotic night life after WWII and especially with the British Forces. It developed even further into social depravity when US servicemen took R&R in Hong Kong during the Vietnam War. When I arrived in 1971, the Vietnam War was still ongoing and thousands of US war veterans were given leave in Hong Kong. The British Forces were also still very present, although numbers had reduced following the demise of National Service.

Wan Chai for service personnel was the place to be. Before entering many of the bars in Wan Chai, punters (customers) were expected to purchase tickets at the entrance. Tickets were usually on sale at 2 HKD (Hong Kong Dollars). Tickets were given in exchange for goods. For example: one ticket would get you a beer, two tickets and you could have a shot of a spirit and of choice of mixer, three tickets would get you a sandwich, four tickets and you were provided with a bowl of fried rice and five tickets would be the price for a 'girls' drink. As you can imagine, at the early part of the night, only one or two tickets were exchanged for a beer or a short; no one ever seemed to exchange three or four tickets but by the end of the night many customers were exchanging five tickets just to have one of the 'Yum Yum's' come sit with you. Other favours were on offer at a price and there was an expectation that you would contribute money when floor shows were performed. In each of the bars, single bedrooms were provided for any extras you might want. These rooms were rather dingy, poorly lit and rather smelly and just provided a bed with a mattress.

One evening, Pat O'Sullivan saw me on board and asked if I wanted to join him for a drink later that evening. I had been out drinking with Pat on a number of occasions but found it difficult as Pat was a heavy drinker and I got drunk quite quickly. However, even when I was drunk, Pat would always look after me and made sure that no harm came to me. Pat had a habit of drinking fast and if I tried to keep up with him would soon fall into a drunken stupor. Pat would never leave me, so would pick me up like a rag doll and carry me from bar to bar. That evening, we met heading for the Royal China Fleet club. We settled down to a quiet night of drinking but were interrupted when a group of American GI's called in for a drink. Most Americans were quite loud and in many ways overpowering. They wanted to make friends with us Brits but they lacked the social etiquette that we Brits were accustomed to.

One American came over to Pat and me saying, "Hi fellas, what's going on?"

"Just having a quiet beer," Pat replied.

"You call that beer?" the American guy retorted. "You Brits only drink Ale, that's not what we call beer, you want to try the real stuff. Do you want to drink with me?" the American guy offered.

Well, this was an offer Pat could not refuse. If anyone asked Pat to drink with him, he saw this as an invitation to go on a 'bender'. Pat could drink like a fish and expected any drinking partner to drink as much and at the same speed as him. Pat loved the idea and took the American guy's offer with enthusiasm. Pat and the American guy began to drink, pint for pint, followed by a large whiskey chaser. After a couple of hours and with approximately 15 pints of Ale and chasers, the American guy began to falter and Pat on the other had had just gotten into his stride. When the American fell on the floor, Pat did the gentlemanly thing, picked up the American, sat him on a chair and ordered another round of drinks. Pat was happily drinking and as he drank, he pulled the American's head back, opening his mouth pouring the same amount of alcohol down the Americans throat as he was drinking. After a further hour of drinking, Pat was getting bored. The truth of the matter was that American was not very talkative, being unconscious and not responding to anything. Pat decided that the American was being rude, so picked him up and carried him to 'Pinkies' (Pinkie was a world famous tattoo artist). At Pinkies, Pat sat the American in the tattooist chair, took the Americans shirt off and ordered Pinkie to give the American a tattoo to cover his chest. Still pouring whisky down the American's throat, Pinkie complied with Pat's request and completed a beautiful Union Flag with 'God Save The Queen' written in Time New Roman underneath. The colours were stunning and any British navy guy would have been proud as punch with the result. Having finished the tattoo, Pat then took the American outside, hailed a taxi and sent the guy back to his ship.

The following evening, Pat and I returned to the Royal China Fleet Club to start another evening out. We stayed longer than expected and as the night moved on, the club filled to capacity. By 11:00 pm, the place was heaving and most participants were well intoxicated. At that point, there was an invasion of American GI's who had come looking for the guy who had desecrated the chest of one of their compatriots. Arguments turned into punch ups and within minutes it seemed as if WWIII had broken out. I was drunk by this time, was grabbed by Pat, thrown in a corner of the bar by the pinball machine and told to stay there. I was also given a bottle of Bacardi and was told to protect this with my life. I was so drunk at this time; I fell fast asleep. Early the following morning, I awoke in a daze, still under the pinball machine and still clutching the precious bottle of Bacardi. I crawled out from under the pin ball machine and surveyed my surroundings. The bar was a wreck. Tables, chairs, bottles and glasses were strewed everywhere. There were a couple of Chinese guys attempting to clean up the mayhem and looked in amazement as I emerged.

"Morning," I said, nodding politely to the cleaners and left the building.

I returned to the ship where I was greeted, asked where I had gotten to the previous evening and was made to give in full detail the happenings of the previous night's events. Happily, no one was badly injured and Pat had not been identified as target for the Americans to get hold of. One or two people had been taken outside by Royal Naval Police but had been released after promising not to be naughty boys and with the proviso that they would return directly to their ship.

Each morning on the forecastle whilst in Hong Kong, 'gofer' traders and others would fill the space selling their wares. It was a ritual for those who had been ashore the previous night to recover from their handovers by drinking copious amounts of soft drinks to ease any symptoms one might have accumulated, (my favourite tipple being chocolate milk). After each night out, I would drink at least six bottles of this life restoring liquid with the hope that it would settle my stomach, ease my aching head of making me vomit to sufficiently carry on with my daily routine. Also for sale on the forecastle, were other fine trinkets such as wood and stone carvings; silks; watches and jewellery and all sorts of Hong Kong memorabilia. One seller had brought on board some fine bone china. Having not spent much money the evening before, I decided to purchase a lovely coffee set to send home to my mother (which I still have until this day). The set comprised a coffee pot, milk jug and sugar bowl, and six cups and saucers. The porcelain was so fine and decorative and at the bottom of each cup, a translucent Chinese woman's face. My brother, when he had been stationed in Hong Kong had also purchased a similar tea set from the same purveyor some twelve years earlier. The items were carefully packed and shipped to England. This purchase was highly treasured by my mother as the tea set bought by my brother had sustained considerable damage over the years after she gave my brother's tea set to his wife and this time. My mother was determined to ensure that the same fate did not happen to the coffee set.

More runs ashore saw more tattoos being applied (I ended up with three more tattoos, of which, none were of my choice), more purchases of exotic gifts for family and friends were bought and some items that had no purpose at all began to accumulate in my locker. I recall going shopping one day with a group of guys, many who were buying for their mothers, wives and girlfriend. Beautiful silks were purchased, dresses and wigs. *Why wigs?* At that point I had no idea why anyone would want to purchase wigs, but then again, this was my first Far Eastern tour, so had no idea why wigs would be needed. I would find out more later during our voyage. We also had handmade shoes made, along with shirts, suits, trousers and jackets. It was fascinating having clothes made to measure. When being fitted for shoes, you would be asked to take off the shoes you were wearing, stand on the open pages of an A4 book, while having your feet traced. You then chose the style you preferred, the colour and the type of leather to be used. I remember having a pair of light brown brogues made. Having these shoes always reminded me of my father, who had died when I was only 11 years old. My father would wear with pride his brown brogues on special occasions and always kept them highly polished. The shoes were collected the following day and fitted like a glove. They were so comfortable and lasted me for years. Shirts, suits and jackets were also made within a day, the tailors carefully measuring, cutting, pinning and sewing to ensure that everything was a perfect fit. After collecting these items and wearing them, one always felt as if you had had them made in Savile Row London.

After being in Hong Kong for two weeks, I was glad to return to some form of normality. I had loved being in Hong Kong but I doubt that I could have survived longer had we stayed. We sailed from Hong Kong on 11 October 1971 heading back to Singapore. We sailed south through the South China Sea passing Vietnam, the Paracel Islands and Spratly Islands. Once at sea, we encountered Typhoon Hester. Typhoon Hester developed over the South China Sea, built over southern China resulting in Hester turning north westward and accelerating. It reached a forward speed of 20 mph, twice the climatological average for typhoons in that region during October. The storm developed an eye before reaching its peak intensity as a category two typhoon. The estimated peak winds to have reached 105 mph. Hester subsequently made landfall near Hue, South Vietnam. Once onshore, the storm's structure rapidly degraded as it weakened. The storm later dissipated over central Laos. Regarded as one of the most destructive storms to strike Vietnam since 1944, Typhoon Hester caused considerable damage in the country and disrupted the Vietnam War. Making landfall directly over the United States military installation in Chu Lai, Hester damaged or destroyed 75 percent of the structures in the base. Sustained winds and gusts in the base were estimated to have reached 80 mph and 105 mph respectively. Four hangars collapsed in the Chu Lai airbase, with total aircraft losses amounting to 36 destroyed and 87 damaged. Losses from the destroyed helicopters exceeded $3.6 million (1971 USD). Dozens of barracks were damaged in Chu Lai and communications were hampered. The 91st Evacuation Hospital was mostly destroyed and was forced to transfer patients to Quy Nhõn. Nearly 50 percent of the structures at the Marble Mountain Air Facility were damaged by the storm's high winds. Heavy rains accompanied the storm, peaking at 5.44 in at Camp Eagle, causing considerable flooding in the country. Approximately 230 miles of coastline between Quãng Tri and Dã Nãng were inundated. About 90 percent of homes in Dã Nãng were damaged. Flooding from the storm washed out a bridge between Fire Support Base Birmingham and Camp Eagle, temporarily isolating two units within the 94th Field Artillery Regiment. Albion cruised through the Typhoon luckily only sustaining minor damage. However, from the onset of the typhoon, everything on board that was loose had to be battened down, locked away or secured. Experiencing such weather conditions is always something that will remain with me. We arrived Back in Singapore on 15 October.

Chapter Thirteen
Farewell to Singapore

Entering Singapore for the last time was a time of joy but also a time of sadness. Soon I was going to leave my spiritual home and I would have to say goodbye to Liu's family. I had already said my farewells to Liu who was now undertaking his basis training in the Singapore Forces. Saying goodbye to Liu's mother and father was going to be hard, as they had welcomed me into their home as a son and had treated me with so much love, respect and kindness.

This was also going to be a very busy time for the ship. For the next two weeks, we would be storing the ship for the next long journey, embarking 40 Commando Royal Marines and 848 Naval Air Squadron as part of the British withdrawal from the Far East and taking part in a number of farewell parades to mark the withdrawal of all British armed forces represented in Singapore. The whole of the naval base was to be handed over to the ANZUK forces and the dockyard was to be officially handed over to the Singapore authorities. HMS Albion was to spearhead a salute of 20 ships and helicopters aboard would take part in an official fly past.

Not having much time to spend ashore, my first port of call was to see Liu's family. The family had understood that this was to be a difficult time as they had not only lost their birth son, they were also preparing to say goodbye to their adoptive son. When saying goodbye to Chinese friends, Chinese gifts play a major role. This not only demonstrates respect to elders and superiors but also to show commitment and enthusiasm towards maintaining close relationships with family and friends. It is difficult to choose gifts when saying goodbye because certain gifts show a lack of respect. The Chinese have a connection-centred culture; the importance of connections lies in 'trust'. People like to build their relationships of trust, therefore, the giving of Chinese gifts is vital to maintaining lasting relationships, particularly if it is tough to sustain those relationships over a long period of time. In such a relationship, one should not give gifts that have sharp edges as this symbolises a 'cut off' of a relationship. Giving sharp objects that are used to cut things suggests that you want to sever a friendship or relationship. So you should never give a knife or scissors as a gift to Chinese people, especially the ones you care about. Neither should you give anything that has a number four associated with it or something that comprises four items. The number four when pronounced in Chinese sounds the same as the word 'death'. Shoes should also not be given as shoes represent 'evil' and is representative of someone running away. Handkerchiefs and clocks are also considered bad luck. Food and fruit is seen as a positive, but even here you have to be careful what fruit is given. Pears in particular should not be given because the Chinese word for pear sounds similar to the word parting. Flowers are for funerals, so too is anything that is black or white and umbrellas represent break-ups and mirrors reflect ghosts. Candles and stone wear are also offensive. Choosing a gift would be difficult as I wanted to give the family something they could remember me by. The Chinese do like to accept local wines but these have to be the more expensive type. Flavoured teas, exotic coffee and kitchen gadgets are also acceptable. Hats, gloves, scarves or clothes are good gifts and I knew that this would be welcomed because of the familiarity of our relationship. So, before visiting Liu's parents, I bought items of clothing that I saw fit and which I knew they would appreciate. Liu's parents gave me the greatest gift in that they organised a banquet. Usually, a banquet is a welcoming gift and they saw my returning as a welcome but also as a farewell. The Chinese do not say goodbye but use the term 'see you again'. My final day with Liu's family was enjoyed with them preparing the banquet and having friends over to wish me well in my journey. I still hold dear this ideology in that I prefer never to say goodbye but only 'see you again'. The banquet was unbelievable. Liu's mother had prepared beef, chicken and pork dishes, fish, seafood, rice, noodles, vegetables and fruits. My favourite lychees had been picked from a tree in the garden and were served in a sweet syrup. The extent of this banquet was one usually given to very close family and I felt privileged to have been thought of as a member of their family. There were tears as I left but I had been filled with happiness from my experiences with Liu's family.

I also had to say my goodbyes to Big Angie and the other Kaytai's who worked in Bugis street. The over dramatics of the Kaytai's, especially Big Angie had to be seen to be believed. They were wailing and crying one minute, smoothing me with hugs and kisses and the next minute were running to meet one of their regular punters.

Suddenly as if switching off a light, tears would stop, dry up, and a quick "See you later" was shouted as they scampered off in pursuit of their business. Big Angie made sure that I had plenty to drink and had ordered a taxi for me to return to Sembawang, all paid for and with a warning to the taxi driver to make sure that 'her Cherry Boy' was safe.

Other days were spent buying presents for home. Watches, cassette recorders were popular. I also had a plate made for my sister-in-law. In the centre of the plate, a photograph of my nephew and niece which had been taken from a 'black and white' photograph then coloured in some miraculous way to look natural. Shopping complete, I gave myself time to visit places that held special memories, like Changi beech, Sembawang Park, Nisoon, China Town, Little India and the waterfront. Time was going far too quickly and it was with a heavy heart I visited these places.

The final place where I had to visit to say goodbye was to the bars and restaurants in Sembawang village. Over the course of being in Singapore, I had met a number of people who had impacted on me greatly. I called into the bars which I frequented saying my goodbyes to the bar staff and to the girls then to the open air food outlet to say my goodbyes to Mohammed and his son Hussein. Hussein was particularly upset at the thought of our leaving. We had become firm friends, albeit I only ever saw Hussein when visiting his father's restaurant. Hussein cried and hugged me asking me to promise to come back to visit him, but I could not give this promise, instead I told him that I would do my best to come back one day and that hopefully our paths would cross again.

The last few days in Sembawang were in preparation for the final withdrawal and salute. The marines were safely embarked, helicopters stored and readied for their final fly past and we were stocked up, re-fuelled and well prepared. We had to rehearse for the guard of honour on the dockyard, accompanied by the marines and the Royal Marine Band.

On 29 October 1971, ratings amassed with the marines on the dockside in Singapore dockyard. We were all looking resplendent in full dress uniforms and the band rang out. We marched with such pride, happy to be journeying home but sad in leaving this wonderful country. The greatest sadness was because this was the end of an era for the British Forces in Singapore and the fact that no other British naval personnel would ever have the privilege to enjoy the hospitality of Singapore in quite the same way that we had. The salute was taken by Air Chief Marshal Sir Brian Burnett and the flyby was spectacular. I understand that many thousands of Singaporeans had watched as the aircraft flew over Singapore and the Naval Base was officially hand over. In the striates, on the following morning, over 20 ships formed to take their final 'steam past' led by HMS Albion. All ships performed procedure alpha, lining their decks with ratings and officers in full uniform. To be involved in this proceeding was something very hard to describe, but for the many thousands of people who had gathered on the shore line, the sight must had been mesmerising. We finally took leave of Singapore heading west. There was not a dry eye on the flight deck of the Albion as we left. Never again would there be the runs ashore that we had. Singapore during the mid to late 1970s began to change dramatically. New infrastructure, extensive building programmes and a 'clean up' of Sembawang and Bugis Street would change the face of Singapore and of its economics. Never did I think that it would be fifty years before I would return to reminisce of these times but when I did return, the memories of my time in Singapore would come flooding back.

Chapter Fourteen
Paradise, Adventure and War Games

From Singapore we headed north, up the western side of Malaysia and then to the east of Indonesia into the Andaman Sea then West at the southern part of the Bay of Bengal. We turned west passing the Nicobar Islands then into the Indian Ocean heading towards the Maldives. Our first port of call sailing west was to the Island of Gan. Gan is the southernmost island of Addu Atoll (previously also known as Seenu Atoll), as well as the southernmost island of the Maldives. It is relatively large by Maldives' standards. The origin of the word 'Gan', comes from the Sanskrit word 'Grama', meaning 'village'. Gan is the second largest island of the atoll, after Hithadhoo, and measures only 0.87 sq miles in area. Gan was formerly inhabited, but its inhabitants were moved to neighbouring islands after the British naval and airbase was built. It has had continuous human habitation since very ancient times. There were large cultivated fields of yams, manioc and coconut palms on this island. A former Havitta at the island's east end had to be removed to build the British Forces runway. Located in the middle of the Indian Ocean, Gan had played a major role during WWII and had been a midway point to Singapore and the Far East. However, like in Singapore, military activities here were being disbanded. By the end of 1971, the RAF Far East Air Force was closed as the major rationale for Gan was gone. Traffic was now much less frequent but the base still remained open for a few more years. By 1975 British military aircraft using the base were an extreme rarity. RAF Gan was thus closed and on 1 April 1976 the island was handed back to the Maldivian Government. At the same time as the RAF use of the airfield ceased, the RAF gained access to the then newly built US airfield 200 miles south of Gan on the British island of Diego Garcia.

Gan Island in the Maldives is an emerald heaven that teems with marine life and immersive cultural experiences. Gan lies just north of the equator. The

Maldives lives up to its moniker of the 'Necklace Islands'. The stunning archipelago comprising 1,200 coral islands and 435 miles southwest of Sri Lanka in the Laccadive Sea. From the air, it is said that these miraculous Islands look like emeralds strewn in a sapphire sea. If ever there was a paradise on earth, the Maldives is the place to be. Beautiful white soft coral beeches ran for mile upon mile, azure blue warm temperate waters and continuous sunshine all added to this jewel of the planet. Runs ashore here were via a liberty boat and time was spent lazing around, getting a rich golden sun tan and enjoying swimming and snorkelling. If ever one wanted paradise, Gan was the place to be. We took food and drink ashore, cooked on open fires and ensured that our presence would not be detected after we left. Somehow, being on Gan also affected everyone psychologically, we felt relaxed, strengthened and at ease with the world. Any anxieties were simply washed away. When leaving, I remember taking time to just watch the atolls disappear in the distance and watched the colour of the sea change from sapphire blue to a darker blue as we moved into deeper waters. Our next pot of call was Mombasa. Mombasa is a coastal city of Kenya and lies along the Indian Ocean. The city is known as the white and blue city in Kenya. It is the country's oldest and second-largest city after the capital Nairobi. We arrived in Mombasa on 14 November, remaining here until 22 November where the ship underwent a week's self-maintenance period (SMP) in Kilinidi harbour.

Mombasa was given up to the British East Africa Association in 1887, the British East Africa Association later becoming the Imperial British East Africa Company. Mombasa came under British administration in 1895. Mombasa initially was the capital of the British East Africa Protectorate and the sea terminal of the Uganda Railway, construction of which was started in 1896. Many workers were brought in from British India to build the railway. Many descendants from these Indian migrants still remain in Kenya. The Sultan of Zanzibar formally presented the town to the British in 1898. Mombasa became the capital of the Protectorate of Kenya, sometime between 1887 and around 1906. The capital was later moved because medical officers warned that the ground was swampy, and urged Sir James Hayes Sadler, the then Commissioner of the East Africa Protectorate, to plead with London to move the town elsewhere to mitigate potential disease. Nairobi has since been Kenya's capital to date.

Entering Mombasa, we were greeted by two sets of metallic elephant tusks which towered over the main road linking together to form an arch. Mombasa's residents were clearly happy to receive British sailors and many stalls began to take route outside the variety of shops that were a permanent feature in the city. Having spent a day wandering the streets and enjoying the hospitality of the city residents, four of us decided that we wanted to be more adventurous and to see some of the wildlife that resided in this part of Africa. We made arrangements to hire a car and to drive along the main road to Nairobi, stopping off at Tsavo to encounter 'Bush' animals at close hand. Tsavo East National Park is one of the oldest and largest parks in Kenya and situated in a semi-arid area previously known as the Taru Desert. The park is located near the town of Voi in Taita-Taveta County of the former Coast Province. The park (Tsavo) is divided into east and west by the A109 road and railway. The A109 being the main thoroughfare to Nairobi. Tsavo is named after the Tsavo River which flows west to east through the National Park; Tsavo boarders the Chyulu Hills National Park and the Mkomazi Game Reserve in Tanzania. Tsavo West National Park is more mountainous and wetter than the East National Park having far more swamps, lakes and natural springs. Lake Jipe and Mzima Springs are home to numerous large animals, including black rhino and an array of bird life. Tsavo East National Park has the Athi and Tsavo rivers converging to form the Galana River. Semi-arid grasslands and savannah make up much of Tsavo East National Park and is considered one of the world's most bio diverse strongholds. Tsavo East National Park is popular to tourists mostly due to the vast amounts of diverse wildlife that can be seen, including the famous 'big five' consisting of lion, black rhino, Cape buffalo, elephant and leopard. The park is also home to a great variety of bird life including black kite, crowned crane, love birds and sacred ibis. Tsavo East National Park is generally flat, with dry plains across which the Galana River flows. Inside Tsavo East lies the Yatta Plateau and Lugarda falls.

On 18 November, our plans began to take shape and we began by collecting our hired car from one of the many car hire companies within Mombasa. We filled the car before setting off with more fuel by way of two jerry cans. We drove through Mombasa to the A109 and began our adventure. We had armed ourselves with an ordinance survey map, plenty of bottled water, beer and food to last several days. It is about 97 miles from Mombasa to Tsavo and we planned to reach our destination within three hours of setting off, taking into account a short stop at Samburu. At our time of travelling, there was a population of around half a million people living in Samburu, made up of four main tribes; colourful and equally distinguishable, each tribe presented in a very proud and upright manner. Here, tribal people had little time for British sailors but welcomed people who spent money. Samburu was also one of the main towns that supported the many villages that sprang off the main road like capillaries. Villagers would merge at such towns to buy essential food stuffs and to exchange bush crafts. Here, young girls would exchange sexual favours with truckers in exchange for a proportion of whatever goods they were carrying. Some drivers would have greater opportunity than others if they were carrying goods that were needed within villages.

After a brief stop in Samburu, we continued our onward journey to Voi. Voi is the largest town in Taita-Taveta County in southern Kenya. Voi lies at the western edge of the Taru Desert, south and west of the Tsavo East National Park. Voi is a market town known for its agricultural and meat products from the fertile Taita Hills. Voi's town centre consists mostly of general stores, shops, markets, kiosks and hotels. Most lodges that service tourists for the national parks are located in the suburbs at the edge of town. After taking a break, we chose to follow one of the tourist trucks to take us into the park. After several miles of following this track, we decided to via off the main track to follow a narrow dirt road in hopes of finding wild animals. After driving a few miles along terrain which was reminiscent of a moon rally track, we stopped to take refreshments.

Our driver Tony 'Sticky' Green was getting a little tired by now and said, "One of you lot are going to have to drive for a bit, I'm knackered."

Us others looked back at amazement at this suggestion as none of us could or had ever driven. Sticky was the only one with a licence. Paul 'Daisy' Adams was the first to point out that he had difficulty walking, let alone driving a car. Equally, Dave 'Bunny' Warren was not keen on taking the wheel, which left only me. As an adventurous spirited type, I looked at the others and volunteered to have a go. And so, after eating sandwiches, cold boiled eggs, snacks, cake and fruit purchased from the NAFFI the previous evening and downing our lunch with a couple of warm beers, I jumped into the driver's seat. This would make a change from sitting in the back of the car but not so comfortable because 'Sticky' was a rather heavy set guy who struggled to get into any of the seats in our hired vehicle. Sticky introduced me to the accelerator, clutch and break and to how the gears worked. Other important parts of the car were not incorporated within this instruction as wipers and indicators would not be essential, especially as we were now miles from anywhere and in the middle of the African bush. Our only distraction was the copious amount of dust that blew, hampering our vision. My driving began with kangaroo hopping, gear crunching, moving at snail pace and over steering. However, after a little while and after lots of shouting by Sticky, Daisy and Bunny, I gradually got into my stride. After about another 30 minutes, my confidence became such that I thought I was a formula one racing driver or and World Class Cross Country Rally Cross driver. I was more relaxed, my co-driver more comfortable and the two back seat drivers almost asleep. All was going so well then *BANG*. Out of nowhere, some kind of gazelle leaped and ran immediately in front of our car. Swerving to miss the oncoming animals and hitting the accelerator rather than the break, I overreacted, over-steered, hit a pothole and rolled the car twice before landing and stopping with the roof of the car lying on the ground and in tall grasses. The roof of the car was now level with the dashboard, all windows had popped and broken and the wheels were still spinning of their own volition. Amazingly, no one was hurt. Sticky had somehow managed to squeeze out of what was left of the passenger window, quickly followed by me. Bunny and Daisy crawled out of the rear window. "Fucking hell," shouted Sticky, "look at the fucking car."

No mention of 'are you OK guys', or is the 'beer safe'; Sticky's main concern was for the car. Actually, it was quite understandable that Sticky was more concerned about the car than he was for the passengers or beer, as Sticky had signed for the car and it was his details the car hire had on record. And secondly, and most importantly, *how the hell were we to get back to Mombasa and the ship?*

Walking in the African bush is not a sensible thing to do unless well prepared. Yes, we had food and water but nothing to protect ourselves from predators, no camping equipment, no proper hiking boots, only shorts, tee shirts and floppy hats. We decided to try to walk back to the main road some miles back taking it in turn to take the lead and take the rear arm. After about two hours walking, and to our luck, we suddenly heard the sound of a truck. Jumping up and down and shouting as loud as we could, we eventually flagged the truck to stop.

We ran to the truck to be greeted by a very irate white game keeper, who shouted, "What the fuck are you doing here? Don't you realise there are dangerous animals in this part of the park and why are you dressed like you're all on a Sunday school outing?"

We explained our predicament and kindly asked for assistance. The gamekeeper invited us to jump on the back of the truck with four of his black workers, who were laughing at us as we boarded. On the back of the truck were various parts of an elephant, four elephant feet, two long tusks and most of its internal organs. The smell was wretched and overwhelming. Us matelot's covered our noses and mouth with our hats and tee shirts while the black guys found it rather amusing. There were millions upon millions of flies also hitching a lift as we headed towards the wrecked hire vehicle. After a few minutes at the wreck, the game warden told us that he could not do anything at that point in time but promised to get us to safety and for us to be able to notify the ship of our whereabouts and what had happened to us on our great adventure. We travelled back to where we had been picked up by the truck and them onward to the main track. A couple of miles down the main track we pulled into what we thought to be a game reserve. Little did we know that this area housed wild animals that required some sort of support before being released back into the wild. As we drove around the compound we saw all of the 'Big Five' that were located within the national park and more. This was better than trying to find wild game by driving. We also established that the elephant which had been decapitated and was in the lorry with us had died of old age. The game warden had been made aware of the elephant's death and it was routine to remove the feet and tusks to stop poachers. Apparently, the tusks were legally obtained and so could be sold to fund the animal operation within the park. The feet would be turned into stools and sold to tourists, again quite legally. The offal was used to feed the carnivores being cared for at the reserve. The whole experience was so educational and we learned so much in such a short time.

After dropping off the contents of the lorry, the game warden said, "I expect you guys want to clean up and get some food?"

Never a true word had been said. We all looked bedraggled and smelt of death. The warden walked us through a wooded area then into an amazing garden; at the top of the garden stood a hotel, hidden from sight until now. We were dumbfounded and couldn't believe our luck when we were given rooms to shower and change. We were able to contact the dockyard who then put us through to the ship. Having explained our predicament to the Jossman, we were told to 'Hang Fire' and he would get back to us.

He then had a brief conversation with the game warden who smiled at us and said "OK" to the joss who was on the other end of the phone.

After hanging up, the game warden said, "Well guys, it looks as if you will be staying a couple of days' courtesy of the Royal Navy. You already have your rooms, dinner is at eight and the bar is open until midnight. Whatever you need, just ask, but remember that there are a number of very influential guests staying her, so behave."

We thanked the game warden and made our way to the bar. It was surprising just how quickly news of our incident had gone around the hotel.

The bar tender welcomed us and said, "I'm glad you guys were not injured in your crash; you were very lucky."

We thanked the bar tender for his concern and best wishes, then took our beers outside to the terrace. This hotel was better than we could have dreamed of. Tables were set around the pool area and one of the waiters told us that we had a table reserved outside for dinner. We felt like film stars, people coming up saying hello then asking us to tell our story. We must have told our adventure at least 15 times, always adding to the story as we went along. Finally, we headed to bed, exhausted by the events of the day but still worried about how we would get back to the ship and the reception we might receive.

The following morning, we were asked to contact the Joss as soon as possible. It took quite a while to locate the Joss but once we made contact he told us that we would be picked up the following day and that he would be in touch again. We were quite surprised at just how understanding the Joss had been and were happy to know that we had another full day in this amazing place.

Loyk Tsavo Camp was a five-star accommodation set miles from anywhere and really gave a sense of being in the wilds of Africa. We spent the morning swimming and lazing around the pool area and during the afternoon took time to visit the animals located within the sanctuary. Lions, cheetahs, leopards, elephants, Cape buffaloes and black rhinos were all housed here and we were allowed to help feed these animals. Giraffes, antelope and zebra also wandered around the enclosure. This had to be the best experience of our trip. Within the hotel, there was a shop that sold traditional craft. I purchased a few gifts for home, carved animals of antelope, rhinos and elephants and a drum made from a hollowed out tree covered with zebra and antelope skin. Our evening was spent relaxing around the pool waiting for news from the ship. At around 2200 hours, we finally got a call from the Joss and were told that our transport would collect us the following morning at 0930 hours and that we had to be ready to move immediately when our transport arrived.

The following morning, we showered, dressed had breakfast and went outside to await our transport. We were expecting a taxi at best or some jeep from the dockyard. To our utter amazement, a Wessex 5 Helicopter could be seen flying towards the hotel. The helicopter landed in an open area just outside the hotel. We moved to where the helicopter had landed and one of the aircrew came towards us.

"OK guys get on board and where's the car?"

The game warden also came over and spoke with the pilot. We thanked him for his generosity and asked him to thank his staff. We waved our farewell and gave an indication to the pilot as to where the car might be. However, the game warden who had come to wave us off had already given the exact location. After just a few minutes, the car was located and the helicopter landed close by. The air crew got out, assessed the situation, returned to the helicopter, took out webbings and other tackle, strapped these to the vehicle and then to the helicopter which was hovering now over the crash site. We lifted the car leaving Tsavo in a Wessex five helicopter, with four gob smacked naval ratings on board and carrying a totally wrecked car underneath us. We flew to Mombasa where the helicopter hovered over the road where the car hire shop was located and proceeded to drop the car outside the shop.

The ship had already departed from Mombasa and the helicopter landed on the flight deck while at sea. Surprisingly, nothing was said about the incident and we carried on with our duties. However, Mombasa had not finished with me yet. Two days later, I was asked if I would like to join with the marines to take part in an exercise ashore. There were only two matelot's who were selected to go with the marines for this exercise. I was joined with Dickey Flood, a stoker from Yorkshire. We were told to pack equipment to last for two to three days and to report to the hanger deck. We collected other equipment for land based activities; a bivouac, sleeping bag, twenty-four ration packs, an SLR (Self Loading Rife) and cooking equipment. In the hanger deck, we joined a contingent of Royal Marines who were already set to fly into the bush and back into Tsavo. We took off from the Albion flying over the sea and on into Tsavo. Flying towards our destination we could see some of the wild life running free and scattering at the noise of the helicopter as we flew overhead. After about a 40-minute flight, we were dropped in an open plain. We unloaded our equipment and went on foot to an area where a few trees had grown and where there were numerous scrub bushes growing. In the distance, a few mud huts stood in a collection and some of the occupants appeared fixated with the activities that were going on around them. We set up camp and after lighting fires cooked our meal using the ingredients taken from the twenty-four-hour ration pack. Darkness drew in early within the African bush and Floody and I were ordered to report to the commanding officer. The commanding officer, a Captain Le Measurer, told us that our task was to become sentries, and we were to walk along a dirt track looking out for members of his team who had gone out previously and who were testing out new navigational equipment. This equipment we were told apparently took guidance from the stars and would be used like a GPS (Global Positioning System) to guide the marines back to camp. We were taken to the dirt track and told to start approximately 150 yards apart, march toward each other and to continue marching covering the distance as instructed. We were also told that we should not march together but should keep our eyes peeled and immediately report to the Captain as soon as we had sight of the marine group. *How naive, could we be?* There was no such guidance system being tested and the purpose of the exercise was actually a stalking exercise. The marines had been instructed to take the camp without the knowledge of those remaining. Floody and I did as we were instructed and began marching up and down this dirt track looking out for the marines. To be in total darkness in the African bush is quite scary. Your mind plays tricks on you and you imagine all sorts of things are happening around you. The trees and bushes were mere silhouettes in the blackness but the night sky was peppered with thousands of stars. My nervousness was beginning to affect me and after about an hour, at the farthest end or our parameters, I thought that I heard something rustling in the bushes. As I met Floody in the middle of our marching area, I told Floody that I thought that I had heard something but that I had not seen anything. Floody told me not to be so stupid, but I could tell that he too was unnerved. At that point, I took out a packet of 'Spangles' (boiled sweets) that I had in my ration pack and shared its contents with Floody. I told Floody that I was going to go against orders and was not going to walk by myself. I told Floody that it was best to investigate together; after all, there could be a pride of lions hiding in the bushes or possibly some warring natives waiting to attack. Clearly, I was not as brave as I thought I was. Both Floody and I moved nervously together trying to establish if there was anything that could endanger or lives or something we could legitimately report to the captain. The next thing we knew, we had been jumped on by some of the marines who had been stalking us and who had now thrown Floody and I to the ground. The Marine who had floored me had his full weight on my prone body and his hand firmly over my mouth. He had hit me so hard that my nose was bleeding and he had split my lip. I was finding it difficult to breathe and spat my spangles into the marine's hand.

"What the fuck?" the marine whispered.

"They're Spangles," I replied, "I couldn't breathe."

"Shut the fuck up," the marine instructed, then pulled me up dragging me into the darkness. At the same time, another marine had jumped on Floody, had rolled him into a ditch, pushed a thick twig into his back and told Floody that he had a knife in his back and that if he made any sound he would be dead. The marine then proceeded to tie wadding around Floody's hands, wrists and feet and using a gag, proceeded to make Floody immobile. The marine then pushed one side of the wooden stake into the side of the ditch then rolled Floody onto the stick. Floody believed that this stick was actually a knife and feared for his life. Floody was left whimpering in the ditch and his marine then joined with my marine where the continued to drag me away from the camp. After a considerable distance, I was told that I was their hostage and had to follow their command. Other marines then returned to the camp and after securing the camp as their own, brought me back into the throng. Having been released, the marines were debriefed and we settled down to have drinks, supper and to discuss the exercise in detail. I went to wash the combination of blood, saliva and spangle juice off my face and then suddenly remembered Floody.

"Oh my god," I shouted. "Where's Floody?"

In the excitement, we had completely forgotten about Floody who was still tied up securely with the stick in his back down in a ditch. When Floody was found and released, he was severely shaken and his dirty face had marks running down where his tears had cleaned his cheeks as they ran down. Floody soon calmed after being given hot chocolate, swore never to volunteer again for such exercises. We chatted for hours before settling down. After a restless night, the camp breakfasted; we packed up and awaited our transport back to the ship. The story about me spitting spangles out when being captured became a laughing point and thereafter, my nickname became 'Spangles'. The marine who had captured me never forgot and each time we met afterwards, he would shout "Hi ya Spangles" and laugh.

From Mombasa and its coastal waters, we were ordered to set sail to the Persian Gulf.

Chapter Fifteen
Withdrawals, Humanitarian Aid, Christmas at Sea and New Year in South Africa

We travelled north through the Indian Ocean and up to the Arabian Sea sailing towards the Persian Gulf. We had been directed to help with a military withdrawal from Masirah Island. Masirah Island is an island which is about 15 miles off the East coast of Oman in the Arabian Sea. Masirah is approximately 40 miles long by 10 miles wide at its widest point and four miles wide at its narrowest point. During the 1930s, Masirah was one of many staging posts between the RAF bases strung across the world, this one being essential for aircraft flying between bases from Iraq to Aden including those in northern Saudi Arabia and along the Arabian Gulf coast, or the Persian Gulf as it was then. Masirah was first used by the British military in the early 1930s. Aircraft landed here to refuel from points south, such as Aden and Salalah, when going to and from Muscat. The base grew until the 1970s supporting British and Oman forces, particularly during The Dhofar Rebellion and providing transit facilities for long distance RAF flights to the Far East. The Dhofar Rebellion, also known as the War in Ghofar or the Omani Civil War, in the province of Dhofar and against the Sultanate of Muscat and Oman. The Dhofar Liberation Front, aimed to create an independent state in Dhofar. The rebels also held broader goals of Arab Nationalism which included the ending of British influence in the Persian Gulf region. The war initially took the form of a low level insurgency with guerrilla warfare being waged against Omani forces and the British presence in the country. In 1970, the Omani coup d'état led to the overthrowing of Sultan Said bin Taimur by his son Qaboos bin Said who was backed by British military intervention. The British were significant in changing the 'hearts and minds' of people to move away from communist ideologies, and began the process of modernising the Sultan of Oman's Armed Forces. During 1970 Britain deployed the SAS (Special Air Services) to conduct anti-insurgency operations against the rebels. The war ended with the final defeat of the rebels in 1976. The BBC also had a presence on the island, a relay facility consisting HF and MF broadcasting transmitters. The Dhofar conflict also resulted in the need for Royal Navy support which at this time was provided by HMS Albion and several other smaller vessels. The withdrawal of military personnel meant that air operations were frequent and heavy. The ship was unable to dock and had to keep moving from place to place. We below decks were kept busy ensuring that the ship could respond at any time to any difficulties that arose or to any potential threats to the ship and air support. Then on 10 December, we were ordered to steam at full speed to the Bay of Bengal to provide aid to United Kingdom citizens in East Pakistan. A was between India and Pakistan had broken out and in response. We steamed at full speed south down the Arabian Sea to the west of India around Sri Lanka and then north up the Bay of Bengal to what is now Bangladesh.

At the time, the Indo-Pakistan war was raging. The Indo-Pakistan war of 1971 was the shortest war in history lasting only 13 days in total. The war was a military confrontation between India and Pakistan that occurred during the liberation war in East Pakistan. Before the end of this very short war, we had been able to evacuate a large number of British citizens to safety before the fall of Dacca but were ordered to leave the Bay of Bengal due to political pressures. We then set sail again from the Bay of Bengal to the Indian Ocean and once again headed for Gan. On reaching Gan, five days later, we disembarked civilians and 40 Royal Marine Commando who were then flown home to the United Kingdom. For the ship, we were to spend Christmas at sea. However, we were given the luxury of two more days on the sun blessed beaches of Gan where we celebrated by having an Al fresco party and barbeque. Leaving Gan for the last time was exactly the same as the first. It felt compulsory to watch as the atoll disappeared into the distance and to see the water change. It somehow felt that we were watching the end of the earth, knowing that we would never see this place in such a pristine condition again. Dolphins led us into deep water, diving in the wake of the ships waves, the dolphins moving at a colossal speed and occasionally turning in full flight. 'Wondrous' is a term that springs to mind, but the term is not sufficient to describe the feeling we had. We were in awe as a wave of euphoria filled our bodies.

With all of the activities that had been going on, we had to remain at sea until we were allowed to dock in Cape Town South Africa, which would not be until New Year's Eve. Christmas at sea in the Indian Ocean is nothing like Christmas at home. One overriding factor is that the weather is much warmer, and work duties had to continue as normal. However, the Christmas spirit was not lacking and the guys in the mess and all messes on board decorated their living spaces with streamers and homemade Christmas trees. Not to be outdone, the catering department also began preparing for Christmas activities and time was set aside for celebrations to take place on the flight deck. It had been difficult for many, particularly those guys who had children at home. Letters had been few and far between and the fact that we could not wish our loved ones a Merry Christmas was a little disheartening. However, paper decorations were being made, trees were being shaped and baubles made. Royal Nay Sailors are ingenious when it comes to making stuff. Toilet rolls were turned into colourful garlands, four sweeping brush heads, and six deck scrubber heads were turned into a tree, baubles were made from old beer cans and even tinsel was cut from beer cans, which was a long and laborious task.

On Christmas Eve I was on duty Afternoon, First and Morning, finishing my shift at 0800 on Christmas morning. I was given Christmas day off and had to start my next shift at 1600 on Boxing Day. Going on watch on Christmas Eve was not so difficult. There was a slight buzz in the air, knowing that tomorrow was Christmas day. None of us would be getting presents from home, or so we thought and the only Christmas cards were those sent from opposite numbers who lived within the mess. Each mess had been saving and accumulating extra beer rations and one or two bottles (possibly scores) of spirit had been smuggled on board. We had also brought copious amounts of 'goodies' including chocolate, snacks, cake and the like and had stored these, along with the smuggled booze in spare lockers. Unfortunately, I was not able to partake in any of the drinking that went on during Christmas Eve, but did have time to fill myself with chocolate and snacks in between watches. As the evening progressed, a greater feeling of expectation could be felt within the lower decks. Steak, roast duck, salmon, lobster and scallops were on the menu for diner. This was followed by Rum Baba's, Brandy Snaps filled with cream, chocolate torte and lemon tart. Crackers were also given out at the serving hatch to add to the spirit of Christmas. Several of the guys who were not working got very pissed and had to sleep it off before they started their watches the next day. At 0400, and at the start of the morning watch, the duty POME of the boiler room fished out a bottle of whiskey from one of the containers holding ice. We drank to each other's health, to the health and wellbeing of the crew, to the ship and Captain and last but not least we toasted the Queen. The bottle of whisky lasted the night but by 0800, not a drop was left. Although not drunk at this point, my head was not that clear and it took some time for me to climb the ladder to the airlock and even more time to get through the airlock and to reach the main deck. Not having any breakfast after drinking half of the night and then to be invited to various messes for a Christmas tot is not a good idea. My first invitation was to the CPO's mess where I was able to keep some decorum. Then on to the POME's mess, where on leaving, I actually fell out of the door way. Then to one of the Seamen's messes, the Leckie's mess and finally by mid-day into one of the Marine's messes. I can barely remember entering the marines mess, but when I woke up, I was totally drenched. What happened to me no one would say, but being so wet, I can only imagine that water was thrown over me to try to wake me up. I did manage to get to the showers and was able to undress at the same time as taking my shower. I made my way to my mess where I slept until around 1800. I was woken up by a couple of the guys who asked if I was going for dinner. I dressed and went for Christmas Dinner, the first food that I had all day. The spread for dinner was awesome, roast turkey, beef, pork and lamb, all of the traditional trimmings and a plethora of vegetables. For sweet, there was trifle, exotic fresh fruit salads, Christmas pudding with Brandy sauce, custard or cream and Christmas cake.

After dinner, and once the galley mess had been cleared, we watched two Fred Quimby produced Tom and Gerry cartoons, (Good Old Fred) and Holiday Inn (White Christmas with Bing Crosby and Danny Kaye). After which, we sang a few carols and then launched into traditional naval songs, including Zulu Warrior, then back to the mess where we continued singing, drank beer and played board games. At around midnight, the leading Killick walked in with a huge box wrapped in Christmas paper. To our surprise, letters and gifts from home had arrived and were duly given out. I reckon everyone on the mess was crying, particularly when reading letters from home. Some letters had been posted three weeks earlier and the later ones about a week earlier, so everyone had at least five or six letters to read. I think I must have read my letters ten times over. I also received a parcel from my mother. She had sent me a white Aran seaman's Jumper. It was exquisite but I would not be able to wear this until we were out of the tropics. Christmas Day had been a great day, albeit we were far from home and at sea.

Boxing Day and I woke early. Had breakfast and was going to make the most of the day before starting my watch at 1800. Boxing Day had been set aside for fun and frolics. The Flight Deck had been transformed. A large canvas swimming pool had been erected, a band stand set up, Fun Fair Stalls built a stage and a games area laid out. After breakfast, I was formally told that I would be representing the stokers mess in the Miss Albion Competition. I was to be dressed and made up by the guys in the mess and would be chaperoned by the biggest, fattest, ugliest and oldest stoker rating on the ship. There was no argument about it, I had been nominated and chosen officially (without my knowledge) to take on this role. Others from the communications mess, Leckies, mess, seamen's mess, cooks mess, steward's mess, weapons mess, airy fairy's mess and deck monkey's mess all had their representatives. Getting ready for the Miss Albion competition was no mean feat. Wigs from Hong Kong, dresses from Japan, makeup from Singapore, jewellery from Australia and the Philippines were all brought out in preparation. Even eyelashes and false nails and adhesive were on hand; now I understood why wigs were being purchased in Hong Kong.

It was no fun being a contestant for the Miss Albion competition. The weather was far too hot to be wearing anything other than short, but having to wear a wig, dress, makeup and false boobs was just too much. I couldn't even take a dip in the pool until the competition had been judged. I was escorted around the fight deck by my chaperon who insisted that I should have a go on all of the fairground stalls, hooking ducks (not the Pilipino type), having a go on the coconut shy, playing darts and sticking cards, as well as tombola and throwing wet sponges at departmental officers. I was restricted from having a go at any of the sports on offer as high heels were banned. Food was being served after the judging of Miss Albion and then I would be able to get changed and enjoy the festivities. The Royal Marine Band played Christmas songs and medleys of current popular music hits. One or two of the guys sang and there was even dancing. At the point of Judging, all competitors were lined up to do a catwalk. Some looked like old washer women and the younger guys participating were quite glamorous. The candidate from the Leckies mess looked stunning. His hair styled (mine was just blond and long) and he wore a red silk Chinese style dress.

His boobs had been fashioned from two balloons filled with water which gave a gentle sway as he walked and his makeup was immaculate. Although I was a contender, it soon became clear who would win. Being second in this prestigious pageant was something I remember with pride. How many more can say that they had come runner-up in a beauty contest held in the middle of the Indian Ocean. My prize was a crate of beer, which went down well with the other rating of my mess. After all of the frivolity, I was escorted back to my mess, changed and showered before joining the rest of the ships company for food and drinks. Sadly, I had to leave early because of being back on duty and having to complete my watch.

For the next five days, we were at sea heading for Cape Town. We were informed that with luck, we would be in Cape Town by New Year's Eve as planned, but was also informed not to hold our breath, as more incidents were unfolding within the region we were patrolling. As it happened, no incident occurred. We left the Indian Ocean just south and west of Port Elizabeth entering the Southern Atlantic Ocean and happily reached Cape Town on 31 December 1971.

Chapter Sixteen
New Year and Homeward Bound

Cape Town is located on the shore of Table Bay, Cape Town, is the oldest urban area in South Africa being developed by the United East India Company as a supply station for Dutch ships sailing to East Africa, India and the Far East. Table Mountain, Devil's Peak and Lion Head on either side form a dramatic mountainous backdrop enclosing the central area of Cape Town, or what is known as the City Bowl. Occasionally, a thin strip of cloud, known colloquially as the 'tablecloth', sometimes forms on top of the mountain. To the immediate south is the Cape Peninsula which is a scenic mountainous spine jutting 25 mile southwards into the Atlantic Ocean and terminating at Cape Point. Many of the city's suburbs lie on the large plain called the Cape Flats, which extend over 30 miles to the east and joins the peninsula to the mainland. The Cape Town region is characterised by an extensive coastline, rugged mountain ranges, coastal plains, inland valleys and semi-desert fringes. Summer had just started in Cape Town so we were expecting warm sunny weather the whole time we were there. Not being disappointed, the average daily temperatures stayed around 27° C. The City of Cape Town includes the central business district of Cape Town, the harbour, the Company's Garden and residential suburbs. Cape Town, unlike Durban, did not have as many bars but people who wanting to drink alcohol tended to visit hotel bars. As this was New Year's Eve and seeing as many of the ship's company had been given the day off, most of us headed for the hotel bars early. Lunchtime drinking never suited me as I usually need to sleep after a few hours of drinking. Today was no exception. By 1600, I, along with about seven guys from the mess were standing on a hotel balcony shouting to passers-by and wishing then A Happy New Year, we were toasting them with champagne and becoming rather raucous. By 1700, I was fast asleep in one of the hotel's toilets. Although I was not aware, a search party was sent out to find me. At around 1930, I was eventually found by Scotty, who, having being told off by many customers, had searched every toilet within the hotel and had eventually found me by standing on a toilet seat in an adjacent cubicle and had looked over the top of the toilet wall to find me. Unfortunately, Scotty had encountered quite a few people using the toilets before finding me. Having found me, the next problem was to get me out of the toilet. For some reason, I could not open the toilet door and a conversation was held on every possible way a toilet door could be opened. No luck, I was stuck. Scotty managed to get the duty manager, who in turn had to call out the maintenance department. By 2030, I was released after the toilet door had been removed. Scotty and I decided to move on from this hotel and to find the group of guys we had come ashore with. We wandered from hotel to hotel but couldn't find our mates. By 2300, Scotty and I decided it best to celebrate New Year as a duo. As we were wandering towards the next hotel on route a group of South Africans met us in the doorway.

"Where are you going guys?" we were asked.

"We're just going into this hotel to celebrate New Year," we replied.

"What, just the two of you?" they said.

"Yes. We have lost our mates and thought it best to find somewhere to celebrate together," we replied.

"We can't have you celebrating alone, come with us," was their response. Scottie and I were then grabbed by the group, pushed into a taxi and driven to one of the occupant's houses. At the house, belonging to our newly found friend's mother, a New Year's Eve Party was in full swing. Left to our own devises, Scottie and I helped ourselves to drink and food from the barbeque and introduced ourselves to the hosts, explaining how we had met their son and his friends along the way. We had such a great night. Our hosts even providing us with swimwear so that we could use their pool. When it came to midnight, Scotty was dragged in front of everyone and introduced as a real Scotsman and was given the task to propose the toast to the New Year. We began singing *Auld Lang Syne* and everyone joined arms and sang along. Scotty sang his heart out and had tears streaming down his face.

I remember asking him if he was OK, to which he replied, "I just wanna ge home."

I presumed that he wanted to return to the ship but soon realised that he was taking about Scotland. It was the first time anyone had spoken about being homesick and with him saying this; I suddenly felt the urge to see my home and family again. We left the party in the early hours of New Year's Day armed with a gift from our hosts. Both of us had a bottle of whiskey and as we walked back to towards the docks and the ship, we swigged on its contents.

My next time ashore saw me heading towards Table Mountain. The quickest way to the summit is via a cable car, but buses also ran a service taking much longer. The longest route was by foot. I chose to take the cable car. At the summit, I took the opportunity to explore. There were three trails all providing 360-degree views of the city, Atlantic Seaboard and the mountain chain stretching across the Cape Peninsula. It was quite exhilarating to be at the summit and provided a memory which I will never forget.

After just five short days in Cape Town, Albion began her last leg home to England from her Far East tour. On 5 January 1972, we set steam for Portsmouth heading north up through the South Atlantic, crossing the equator and into the Northern Atlantic Ocean. It was to take another 15 days before we were back in British waters but 19 days before we actually docked in Portsmouth Harbour. The speed at which we sailed saw weather changing day by day, particularly as we headed into the Northern hemisphere. There was an excitement about returning to Britain but also sadness with what we had left behind. As we began to travel north, uniforms were swapped from tropical whites to our normal blues. On 20 January, as we approached home waters, 848 Naval Air Squadron was disembarked from the ship. We were planned to enter Portsmouth Dockyard on 24 January 1972 but before this, the ship hosted a family day.

The Families Day is where families and relatives are brought out to the ship by liberty boat and escorted on board to attend a banquet reception. Unfortunately for me, at the time families were arriving and being met by their naval family in the hanger deck, I was still on duty and couldn't meet my mother and her friend until the watch was completed. Having said this, it was me who was more disappointed than my mother and her friend. Apparently, on arrival, my mother was taken to the hanger deck where wine and a buffet was being served. The food which had been prepared was stunning and every dish garnished by the skilful talents of the resident Chinese chefs. Ornate animals, flowers, pots and statues had been carved using vegetables and fruit. Bread had been baked representing a harvest and which had British wildlife surrounding the wreaths of corn and iconic historical architectural buildings had been made out of icing and which stood next to the sweet table. At its centre was a replica of Saint Paul's Cathedral. My mother and her friend were totally taken aback by the sheer skill and ornateness of these garnishes and after asking questions about how each had been constructed had asked if she could take samples home.

When I had completed my watch, I excitedly went to greet my mother. Still in overalls, I found her stuffing various food items into her handbag. After a quick greeting (with lots of tears), I was ordered off the hanger deck to get showered and changed. I returned in evening dress (as was required) and spent a happy few hours with my mother. We spent most of the time talking about the food that was on offer and of the garnishes that she had acquired. There wasn't much time to talk about my many travels, but I did promise to tell her all about my year in the Far East over the next few days while she and her friend were in Portsmouth and as soon as I got home on leave. I provided my mother with information about where to stand to have the best view of the ship sailing into 'Pompey' (Portsmouth) and the best time to be there, given it was January and frightfully cold. My mother, her friend and all of the other families disembarked and were returned back to terra firma to await the arrival of Albion.

On the morning of 24 January, HMS Albion returned to Portsmouth sailing in under procedure Alpha. My mother, along with many of the crew's families had gathered on the Royal Tower on the Southsea side of the dockyard. As we steamed towards the dockyard, we could see the countless hundreds of people who had come out to welcome us back home. Flags were being waved, loud cheers could be heard getting louder and louder as we slowly moved through the home waters and then, the Royal Marine Band struck up with a rousing rendition of Royal Britannia, followed by *A Life on the Ocean Waves, Heart of Oak* and *Sarie Marais* interspersed with the playing of the National Anthem and a call to present arms. It was hard to describe the emotions that we all experienced as we docked; elation, sadness, wanting, joy, anticipation, exhilaration and relief all rolled into one but most of all pride; proud to be home, proud to have served and proud to represent Great Britain and the Royal Navy.

We were to remain in Portsmouth until April 1972 to undergo maintenance and take our long awaited leave, but before all of this, I was able to spend a few days with my mother and her friend who had arranged to stay for a few days on a shopping rekey of Portsmouth and to see what sights there were to see in this historical place.

During the times I had available whilst my mother was in Portsmouth, we met each time. We walked the streets of Portsmouth and Southsea, shopped together, had lunch and dinner together, planned my leave together, caught up on events that were going on at home and I had to provide a rundown of the places that I had visited, what I had been doing and the most memorable moments. I was able to tell my mother much about where we had been and what we had been doing but omitted to tell her all the sordid parts. These few days went far too quickly and soon my mother left to return home stocked with gifts that I had purchased abroad and also with jewellery I had purchased in Portsmouth as a welcoming home gift. I was to take leave two weeks after my mother left and so our parting was not that traumatic.

Being in Portsmouth was so different to being in exotic climes, for one the weather was cold, it seemed to rain consistently and the pubs and bars were not as vibrant or as enjoyable. We had docked on the quay in Portsmouth harbour, a stone's throw from the dry dock where HMS Victory stood. Each day we would see the Victory from the Albion and had to pass Victory in order to leave the dockyard. HMS Victory is possibly the Royal Navy's most famous warship. Victory is renowned for her role in the Battle of Trafalgar as being the flagship for Admiral Horatio Nelson. Although never going to sea again, HMS Victory still played a dual role. Victory is the Flagship of the First Sea Lord and also stands as a living museum to the Georgian Navy. Portsmouth dockyard during the early 1970s was quite a grim looking place, particularly in winter and it always felt good to be able to escape the confines of the dockyard. On leaving the dockyard, most of the naval ratings headed for Commercial Road. There so many pubs along Commercial Road that if you had a drink in each pub, you could guarantee that you would be drunk before you reached the halfway stage. One of my favourite haunts was The Wiltshire Lamb Tavern situated in Hampshire Terrace. There, I was always cared for by the landlord and his wife. The landlord was ex-navy and upon retiring decided to stay in Portsmouth and become a landlord. As soon as I got anywhere near to becoming incapable, the landlord and his wife would always have a taxi on tap to ferry me back to the dockyard. I met some wonderful characters in the Wiltshire Lamb, two of which worked in theatre and who introduced me to a number of well-known celebrities. Peter Jones who worked in the West End of London and John Hart who was the head carpenter with the Royal Ballet. Both lived in Havant but used the Wiltshire Lamb when they were at home. Peter was at home more than John but both had a wicked sense of humour. It was Peter who took me to the Kings' Theatre in Portsmouth where I met such greats as Frankie Howard, Charlie Drake, Clive

Dunn and many other television stars of the day. John introduced me to such people like Sir Frederick Ashton, Sir John Gielgud and Sir Lawrence Olivier. To meet such personalities was mind-blowing and I was quite star struck at the time.

Going on leave was the one thing that I had looked forward to and during the latter part of February I collected my rail warrant for my journey home and to be able to visit home after over a year's absence. I remember the train journey being long and tedious, arriving in Wolverhampton at around 1930 hours. I remember struggling with my suitcase, holdall and with many gifts that I had purchased on my travels thus far and which my mother had not been able to carry with her. Arriving by bus from Wolverhampton to my home town of Willenhall, I immediately made my way to the Prince of Wales, a pub frequented by one of my brothers and where his friends congregated. It was good to see familiar faces and as it was a Friday, the pub was heaving. My brother arrived and by the time we left at around 2300, I had consumed more drinks than I had anticipated, had parted with some of the gifts I had lugged along with me and we made our way home. It was good to see my mother and be in familiar surroundings again but the feel of being home was quite different from what I remembered. Visiting my immediate family members was the pinnacle of my leave. Especially seeing my other four brothers and my nephews and nieces. Going out was strange, people who knew me looked as if I had grown two heads and old school friends looked as if they had aged well beyond their years. I had so many stories to tell but those people I met had very little to say in terms of what they had done since I had left home. Their worlds seemed dull and restricted. Whereas mine had been adventurous and thrilling. I recall one evening going into a local pub having drinks bought for me all night and was a bit worse for wear.

On leaving the pub, one old guy said, "Look at the state of you. They should bring back national service that would have put you right."

I looked at the old guy in amazement, but before I could say anything, my brother piped up, "He's probably done more time in the forces then you ever did and has seen more action than you probably ever have."

The old guy shut up immediately, continuing to consume his pint. This comment made me quite uncomfortable as I began to realise how small and narrow minded my home town neighbours were. I knew that I would never want to be like these people and wanted more out of life than a nine to five existence. I think that my mother was also struggling to see me acting differently. After all, I had left home as a young 16-year-old boy and had returned as a young man. I know that it sounds corny, but I had changed and had done so dramatically. One night, after visiting friends, I called into the pub on my way home leaving around 2200 then made my way home. On route, I saw a figure walking towards me walking a small dog. It was my mother.

As I got closer, I smiled and said, "Hello."

My mother did not look happy and asked, "Where have you been?"

I explained that I had visited friends and that I had called into the pub for one drink before walking home.

My mother said, "Do you know what time it is? It's after ten o'clock."

"Yes," I replied, "it's not late."

"You can't be up to any good being out this late. Only burglars and people up to no good step out this late," my mother said.

Shocked, I also realised that my mother was also stuck in the past and had not recognised that I was older and wiser than I had been when I left home two years previously. After three weeks at home, I was ready to return to Portsmouth and to my ship. It was sad to leave my mother and immediate family but I knew I was ready and willing to absorb other new possibilities. I returned to Portsmouth with some relief but still troubled with what had happened during my leave and the way in which life had stood still for people who lived in my birth place.

More time was spent in Portsmouth with friends and during days off, I spent these with John and Peter and with staying at the Sailor's Rest. When off duty following my watches, I would often wander over to the dockyard NAAFI. Crossing the dockyard at night resembled a science fiction movie. Noises coming from ships, and dockyard machinery provided the backing sound and steam coming from the many pipes crossing from the dockyard boiler house to individual ships provided a strange atmosphere. As winter began to lapse and spring started to awaken, we busied ourselves on board preparing for our next tour of duty.

Chapter Seventeen
Back to the Med

After only three months in the UK and after maintenance and leave, the ship sailed once again from Portsmouth. This time we were heading back to the Mediterranean. On 11 April 1972 and after leaving harbour, we embarked 848 Naval Air Squadron. The ship headed straight to the Mediterranean and for Gibraltar. Returning to Gibraltar was refreshing. The weather was much better than the UK and of course we anticipated Jimmy waiting for the crew to visit his bar. Sadly Jimmy had passed away while we were in the Far East. It had been over a year since we were last in Gibraltar and in visiting Jimmy's bar, but staff in the bar remembered us all by name and welcomed newcomers who had joined the crew in Portsmouth. I know that I had only been to Gibraltar once before but I felt that I was a veteran and was able to point out various sights and bars to the 'greenies' (new crew). The visit to Gibraltar was short and we were soon steaming towards Cyprus. We were to lay off Cyprus for nine days to support the Royal Marines who were to take part in ground exercises. Arriving off the coast of Cyprus on 20 April, I was to celebrate my eighteenth birthday at sea. This was to be my second birthday away from the UK and the second time away from home and family.

Being at sea, I thought that I would not be celebrating my birthday and so set about putting all my efforts into my duties. The day before my birthday I was on watch during the Afternoon, First and Morning. As I entered the boiler room at midnight on the 22 April, the opposite watch and duty POME's all wished me happy birthday. At 0400, I returned to the boiler room to complete the morning watch and this round of duty to be met with blown-up condoms which had been stuffed into the airlock and which had birthday wishes written on them with indelible ink. Faces and phallic symbols were also drawn on the condoms and messages I do not wish to express here now for fear of shocking friends and

152

family. Going out of the airlock and descending into the depth of the boiler room I encountered bunting, balloons and streamers. As I approached the work area, my opposite numbers and the duty POME's began clapping and cheering then burst into song singing Happy Birthday. Cans of beer appeared and everyone drank a toast. Sadly, the opposite watch had to leave to get their rest before returning to take over again at 0800. It was also quite sad that we also couldn't have another drink. Health and safety would have gone ballistic if it had been introduced at that time. Drinking on duty was an offence and punishment could be severe.

At 0800 sharp, the opposite watch returned to relieve us and having wished me Happy Birthday again, we parted our ways for a short time. I returned to my mess where all was quiet, most of my mess mates were by now at their work stations. I went to the locker room removed my steaming boots and overalls, put on my flip flops, grabbed my towel and wash bag, which include washing detergent (Dhobie Dust) and proceeded to go to the showers. It is compulsory that immediately after completing any watch or period of duty everyone must change their underwear and socks and take a shower. Taking a shower was ritualised. First, if a shave was needed, then you shaved first then cleaned your teeth. You then had to change the water in the sink, add washing powder and then hand wash your underwear and socks. These had to be rinsed thoroughly to prevent Dhobie Rash. Then and only then could you shower. As I didn't need a shave, I brushed my teeth and put water in the sink to commence my washing, as I added the washing powder, the water in the sink turned a deep blue. I had already put my 'skidders' (underwear) in the sink along with my socks. I tried to retrieve these items from the sink but found my hands had turned a deep shade of blue. I took my clothing items to the shower to try to rinse them and to remove the dye from my hands, but to no avail. I showered but came away from the showers with ruined knickers and socks and hands that looked as if they were gloved. As I walked to the mess, a number of ratings gave me strange looks noticing my hands. I reached my locker, put on clean clothing and went into the mess. In the time I had taken to get showered and dressed, the whole mess had been decked with posters, more balloons and condoms and most of my mess mates sang *Happy Birthday*. I soon found out who had sabotaged my washing powder and what I needed to do to remove the offending substance from my hands. My mess mates had provided me with a birthday cake and I was handed a number of birthday cards. The mess had to break-up quite quickly as many had snuck off from their work places just to wish me happy birthday. I went for breakfast and then returned to the mess to get some 'shut eye' (sleep). When I woke up, I was greeted with cards from home, a great birthday lunch and a party of sorts during the evening.

The following day, HMS Albion started manoeuvres with a large number of NATO allies. Ships from the UK, USA and France congregated for exercise 'Dawn Patrol'. The navies of Europe and in particular the Royal Navy, made fundamental contributions to the Cold War effort at sea, ensuring an effective deterrent to Soviet naval forces. Soviet naval forces had grown to menacing proportions during the cold war and our task was to show that we could contain a Soviet attack until US forces arrived on the scene (the US forces being the most dominant in terms of ships, equipment and manpower). European navies attempted to take essential niche capabilities which were tailored for their own unique maritime environments. The Royal Navy made important contributions to broader NATO efforts in the high-stakes arenas of sea control, power projection and even nuclear deterrence. What was obvious was that the alliance of European navies succeeded collectively in wielding formidable sea power. Our contribution also aided to the political cohesion that was crucial to an essentially maritime alliance, and we were at the forefront of real operational contributions.

During these operations, we were allowed a few days in Kavala and Souda Bay for R&R. Kavala is a city in northern Greece, and is the principal seaport of eastern Macedonia. Kavala city is situated on the Bay of Kavala, across from the island of Thasos. Strategically, Kavala is connected with all the islands of the Northern Aegean Sea and because of its close proximity to Macedonia, Bulgaria and Turkey played an essential part in deflecting any threats to the NATO alliances from the Russians. Kavala initially was a fishing port but had industrialised, yet still offered typical Greek hospitality. The tavernas were the ratings main point of interest here and offered a relaxing backdrop to the tensions that were being felt at this time in the Mediterranean.

After our short stay in Kavala, we steamed to Souda Bay. Souda Bay is a bay and natural harbour near the town of Souda on the northwest coast of Crete. The bay has a deep natural harbour. It is formed between the Akrotiri peninsula and Cape Drapano, and runs west to east. The bay is overlooked on both sides by hills, with a relatively low and narrow isthmus in the west near Chania. Near the mouth of Souda bay, between the Akrotiri peninsula and the town of Kalives, are a group of small islands with Venetian fortifications. The largest island is Souda Island, giving its name to the bay. Because of the large presence of NATO in this area, there are no formal beaches and therefore permission to use any beeches in this area had to come from the Hellenic authorities. This did not deter us from visiting the local villages of Megala, Chorafia and Kalives, where we were able to again enjoy Greek hospitality and be able to take a swim in the warm waters of the Mediterranean. Sometimes it is difficult to distinguish just what seas you might be swimming in around this area because the Sea of Crete or Cretan Sea forms part of the Aegean Sea which is at the Southern extremity of the Island of Crete. The sea then stretches to the North of the island and east. To the West is the Ionian Sea and to the Northwest the Myrtonan Sea, which is a subdivision of the Mediterranean. To the East-SE the Mediterranean Sea is sometimes called the Levantine Sea and across the island of Crete, to the opposite shore begins the Libyan Sea. It sometimes amazes me to think of all the seas and oceans that I have sailed in, through or circumnavigated but my guess is that I had probably covered the majority of the world's waterways. It was whilst we were in Crete that I completed my full second year in the navy.

Returning west for home, we had another short stop in Gibraltar. This time in Gibraltar, a couple of us decided to explore some of the awesome historical places on the peninsula. We visited Gorham's Cave, which is set in steep limestone cliffs on the eastern side of the Rock of Gibraltar. The cave complex is of particular interest to archaeologists and palaeontologists as these caves hold deposits that provide evidence of Neanderthal occupation. Within the caves, there is evidence of the hunting of birds and marine life for food, the use of feathers for ornamentation and the presence of abstract rock engravings. We also visited St Michael's Cave. St Michaels Cave is located on what is called the Upper Rock, inside the Upper Rock Nature Reserve of Gibraltar and sits at a height of well over 300 metres above sea level. The name St Michaels comes from a grotto, or cave of a similar nature which is located in Monte Gargano, in Apulia Italy, where it is believed that the Archangel Michael is said to have shown himself. We visited the main attraction here known as the Cathedral Cave, which forms part of St Michaels cave and which at one time was thought to be bottomless. It was also thought that this was just one end of a passage that went from the strait of Gibraltar, and which once linked to Morocco. Legend has it that the Barbary Apes or Gibraltar Monkeys entered Gibraltar from Morocco from this passage before seismic events closed the passage. Whether this is true or just a legend, it certainly formed a good basis for making up stories. The Cathedral Cave had been strategically lit in a variety of hues. The colours reflecting on the rocks, stalactites and stalagmites were just breath-taking and the name 'cathedral' seemed to be well given. Mythological stories about Gibraltar add to the mystique of the area. The Rock has long been considered to be one of the Pillars of Hercules and the caves were thought to be the Gates to Hades, or Hell, an entryway to the Underworld where the dead rested. On our way back to the UK, we made another official visit to Brest in France and for seven days we flew the flag of the then Commander-in-Chief Fleet, Admiral Sir Edward Ashmore. I believe that Brest's history has always been linked to the sea and the Académie de Marine is located there. I also understand that the aircraft carrier the Charles de Gaulle was also built there. Brest also holds an international festival of the sea when sailors from all over the world gather to compete in the practice of rigging.

The ship then returned to Portsmouth on 31 May. The crossing was fairly smooth, having a tinge of summer advancing. Arriving in Portsmouth was, for many of us, a sad time, as our captain, Captain James Jungius RN had completed his tour of duty and was leaving the ship. Captain Jungis, whilst serving on HMS Albion became Assistant Chief of the Naval Staff (Operational Requirements). He went on to become Deputy Supreme Allied Commander Atlantic in 1975 and the Supreme Allied Commander Atlantic's Representative in Europe in 1978 before retiring in 1980. In the first week of June, Captain William Staveley RN assumed command. Captain Staveley had seen previous service as a minesweeper commander on coastal patrol during the Indonesia–Malaysia confrontation before commanding a frigate. Captain Staveley then commanded HMS Albion before achieving higher command in the Navy. Captain Staveley later became the First Sea Lord and Chief of Naval Staff in the late 1980s and fought for a fleet to remain large enough to meet NATO commitments.

Chapter Eighteen
Colder Climates

After returning from our second Mediterranean tour, the Albion was given one month to prepare for being in much colder climates. Two weeks leave was given to all ratings allowing us to visit home. I spent much of my leave relaxing and visiting old haunts. I visited my old school at the request of my old headmaster who had bumped into me while shopping. I was paraded in front of the school during their morning assembly and was hailed a fine example of achievement. I was invited to join in with some of the fourth and fifth year classes to offer insight into the Navy as a preferred career choice. Some of my old teachers were quite taken aback when I gave a rundown of the countries and places that I had visited; the pupils were in awe and wanted to know if I had been in any conflicts. I tried to explain the ships role in the Far East, our involvement in the withdrawal from Singapore and Masirah Island and the withdrawal of British citizens from what is now Bangladesh during the Indo-Pakistan war and our role in NATO and the Cold War. Trying to cram so much in was difficult but I left knowing that I had started a deep conversation and potentially had inspired some of the pupils to consider a career in the Royal Navy. My old teachers wanted to know more and so I returned a few times to give them briefings. It was strange to have a different relationship with my old teachers, and placing me on par with them as educators.

I also visited my old college. It had been through a friendship that I had met at college who had inspired me to join the navy. Not because of the career opportunities available but because my college friend had visited the college just after he had joined the navy in his uniform and I was just awestruck with just how smart he looked. I think the second thing that influenced me at that time was the fact that the navy uniform had flared trousers and during the late 60s flares were all the fashion. The opportunity to travel was also a major factor and I saw the navy being the best division of the armed forces to allow for this. Being born on a Thursday (Thursday's child has far to go), perhaps it was inevitable that I chose the navy as opposed to the army or Royal Air Force. Finally, the Navy was and I believe still is, the senior of all services and to have an opportunity to be part of this service was a driving factor too.

I had been involved in some sort of uniformed organisation ever since early childhood. I joined the Cubs when I was six years old, the Boys Brigade at 11 years old and the Army Cadets when I was 13. I seemed that I was destined to wear a uniform as a young adult. During my leave I also revisited those organisations I had been involved with as a child. It was fun to see the children respond to my visit. It seemed as if they wanted to show me how well they could march and carry out drill. I also joined my eldest brother a couple of times at the Royal British Legion. At the time, our local branch and club were one of the largest in the country. My family had been involved with the Royal British Legion since its formation in 1922. My uncles had served in the Army during WWI and had been keen members of the legion, and then my elder brothers were in National Service. They too supported the work the legion provided. Visiting the club was uplifting with many of the members pleased to see me keeping up the family tradition.

My leave this time ended in what seemed double quick time and I returned to Portsmouth refreshed, awaiting what would come next. We remained in Portsmouth until June 1972 when we left port to begin demonstrations at sea for officers from the Royal College of Defence Studies. The Royal College of Defence Studies (RCDS) is the senior college of the Defence Academy of the United Kingdom. The college provides the capstone to the strategic education of officers of the Armed Forces and equivalent civil servants who have the potential to reach the highest ranks and who must therefore understand and be comfortable working at strategic levels in and across-government and international environments. The college originally was the Imperial Defence College, modernising in 1927 in accordance with Winston Churchill's vision of promoting greater understanding between senior military officers, diplomats, civil servants and officials. Students from the Royal College were welcomed on board and were given the opportunity to observe manoeuvres at sea. This was a busy time for all on board as the manoeuvres encompassed reactive drills to hypothetical possibilities. We in the boiler room were responding as required and even had to act to fictional damage events in other parts of the ship. One such event saw our second boiler room being shut down, which had us in boiler room one having to take on the role of two boiler rooms, ensuring the smooth running of the ship. After several days at sea, the students from the Royal College disembarked and the ship headed north for Rosyth.

The Royal Naval Dockyard Rosyth, as was, was situated on the Firth of Forth and undertook the refitting of surface vessels and submarines. Being in the Royal Dockyard Rosyth was very different to Portsmouth or Plymouth as there were far more submarines in dock and even the first British nuclear submarine HMS Dreadnaught. HMS Dreadnaught was the first of the United Kingdom's nuclear-powered submarines commissioned in 1963. The submarine was heavily guarded while in dock and difficult to get close to. The size of this magnificent ship dwarfed the other submarines tied up. A Polaris submarine had a crew of 14 officers and 129 ratings. Every sailor had his own bunk, so they did not have to 'hot bunk' as in other smaller submarines. Meals were also served in a dining hall, rather than having to be eaten in the mess while sitting on bunks. The crew included a doctor and supply officers. Before commencing any patrol, a submarine was stocked with enough food for 143 men. Supplies for a typical patrol might include 3,500 pounds of beef, 5,000 pounds of potatoes, 5,000 eggs, 1,000 chickens, two miles of sausages, and one tonne of beans. Polaris skippers paid great attention to boosting morale on their boats; however, the crew would often become quite low around the fifth or sixth week of a patrol because of being completely submerged for the majority of that time.

While in Rosyth, HMS Albion had a visit from the Grand Duke of Luxembourg. This was the first time that the Grand Duke and Duchess of Luxembourg had ever paid a state visit to the United Kingdom and the first time that a ruler of Luxembourg has made such a visit. The Grand Duke had significant knowledge of the United Kingdom and had served with the Irish Guards during WWII. This state visit was just one of a number of 'European' exchange state visits, building to Britain's entry to European Economic Community (EEC). *(It seems strange that United Kingdom was preparing to become part of the EEC and now at the time of writing, the United Kingdom is leaving the EEC).* While in Rosyth, we embarked 45 Commando Royal Marines and 848 Naval Air Squadron. From Rosyth, we sailed north to the Orkney Islands. Here we carried out exercises with 848 Naval Air Squadron flying 45 Commando on and off the ship. Orkney is an archipelago off the north-eastern coast of Scotland. The Orkney's are made up of 70 islands, of which, 20 are inhabited, with the exception of the rugged island of Hoy and their western coastlines. The Orkneys are mostly low-lying rocks that slope gently to the sea. Unbeknown to the Commando's, the carrying out of exercises in the Orkney's would be a pre-curser to the Falkland's war ten years later. From the Orkney's, and after completion of these exercises, we steamed to Rotterdam where we stayed for six days.

Because Rotterdam was in close proximity to Amsterdam, approximately 37 miles, most of the crew had planned to visit the capital at some point during our stay.

Surprisingly, Rotterdam as a city has many facets. It is seen as a tough port because of its large shipping heritage but was also surprisingly quite trendy too. The night life in Rotterdam was positively buzzing and there were plenty of bars and nightclubs to choose from. It was also a great city for shopping. Unlike Amsterdam, the architecture was modern and it appeared to be changing as there were many building projects going on. I was amazed by how much the Dutch were like the British. They enjoyed their beer and food was similar to home. Even their names were similar to the British; albeit spelt differently, like Luuk; Daan, Thomas, and Peter. I met two brothers from Rotterdam Noah and Max. The brothers invited me to their home along with three other guys who were in my group. I think that we Brits were more socially uncomfortable than the Dutch as our manners overtook us. We all had a feeling that the family wanted us to relax and to treat their home as a family home, but we tended to sit there like guards on duty. The evening was a resounding success in that we were all fed well and the beer flowed constantly. I was fascinated that when the locals spoke in their mother tongue, I could actually follow much of their conversations yet I could not speak a word of Dutch. The Dutch, on the other hand spoke extremely good English as well as French. I was impressed that most people were multilingual, putting us Brits to shame. The people we met were incredibly friendly, inviting many of the ship's company to join them into their homes for dinner and to meet their families.

On another occasion and as planned, a group of us visited Amsterdam. The city was immaculately clean, had wonderful bars that sat along the many canals and of course there was the 'Red Light' district. The red light district was like a magnate pulling British sailors like moths to a spider's web, we were almost trapped once we entered. Because we were in uniform, many of the girls who sat in windows like manikins would call us and invite us to spend time with them. As it happened, I only saw one or two of our ship's company actually take up the girls offer. Most of these guys were new to the ship and had not had the same experiences as some of us 'older' guys. The fascination of being in the red light district kept us drinking in nearby bars and the cost of drinks here was much more expensive than in other city bars.

We also took the opportunity to visit Delft, which was about twenty minutes from Rotterdam. Delft is surrounded by canals and is internationally known as the manufacturing base for Delftware. This hand-painted blue-and-white pottery is sold everywhere in the city and we explored the many small potteries that were scattered around. Delft also had a vibrant and lively market square which provided us with respite and a place to eat and drink. I was astonished by how much I had loved Holland, yet since, have not visited as regularly as I would have liked.

On 8 July 1972, 848 Naval Air Squadron disembarked HMS Albion. This was the last time the squadron would ever be aboard. We sailed from Rotterdam for Greenock to spend a week there. It was Clyde week. Clyde week is a regatta and occasionally, the navy take the opportunity to showcase to encourage young men to join up. It is surprising just how many young Scots become interested in a career in the Royal Navy from such visits. After visiting Greenock, we made our last UK port visit arriving in Dover. Our visit to Dover marked the ships adoption by the Confederation of Cinque Ports. The Confederation of Cinque Ports is a historic series of coastal towns in Kent, Sussex and Essex. It was originally formed for military and trade purposes, but is now entirely ceremonial. The ports lie at the eastern end of the English Channel, where the crossing to the continent is narrowest. The name is Norman French, meaning 'five ports'. These ports are Hastings; New Romney, Hythe, Dover and Sandwich. Having anchored off Dover, this allowed the ship to be adopted. For shore leave, we had to take liberty boats. Our run ashore in Dover went without mishaps and appeared to be without incident that is until we tried to get a liberty boat back to the ship. For some reason, we were not sent a liberty boat to return. Instead where we congregated, lorries pulled up and were told to get on board and that we were being taken to Deal Barracks. Deal served as the headquarters of the Royal Naval School of Music (founded in 1903 to provide Royal Marines bands for ships of the Royal Navy). Deal had been renamed the Royal Marines School of Music after the Second World War, it expanded to provide musical training for both junior and senior recruits for all 36 Royal Marines bands. We were told that we could not return to the ship that night and were told that we had to 'get our heads down' in the Deal Barracks school gym. To see so many of our ship's company in one place at the same time was astonishing. In the gym, several of us decided it was a good idea to find somewhere comfortable. Many of the gym mats has already been taken and so my group thought that the trampoline would be a good place to sleep. Having fixed up the trampoline, about fifty people fought to get a place. The trampoline might hold six at a push, but fifty would have been impossible. Having being in the pubs all evening and some a little worse for wear, soon a punch broke out. While most ended up fighting on the floor, my group managed to take hold of the trampoline. This was like the victory at Trafalgar and we stood aloft, bouncing and cheering as the fight developed. After about twenty minutes or so, one of the Marine officers bounded into the gym and called a halt to the fighting. My gang were made to get off the trampoline and store it securely. We then had to try to find a place to sleep. After the officer had gone, we re-erected the trampoline and managed to get some sleep before being woken up by one of the Marines buglers. We were loaded back on to the transport and back to the pick-up point, then ferried back to the ship. Luckily enough, our escapades of the previous evening were never questioned but the story of the storming of the 'Bastille' (fight for the trampoline) was a talking point for weeks.

On 18 July, before entering Portsmouth harbour, HMS Albion held another Families' Day before going alongside in the naval base for leave and maintenance. My mother of course came along with two of her close friends. I think that my mother had made an impression on her first visit as many of the officers and non-commissioned offers were approaching her to have a chat. My mother must have thought that she had a special status, telling her friends who each person was and how she had met them the first time she had come on board. Even the chefs had made extra garnish for her to take home. My mother and her friends had booked a holiday on the 'Isle of Wight' and I believe that on her return to the hotel, she had the staff preserve her treasured garnishes in their fridges until her return home. When the Albion docked, maintenance began in earnest and leave was given. I, instead of returning home, spent several days on the Isle of Wight with my mother and the rest of my leave was spent hanging around Portsmouth. In September, we set off again, this time for the Arctic Circle.

The Albion was to take part in Exercise 'Strong Express', then the largest NATO exercise ever staged, in Norwegian waters around Haarstad. This exercise involved carriers, cruisers, destroyers, submarines, hover craft and torpedo boats operating in the narrow fiords of Norway. Fighters from carriers and lonely bases on the mainland were flown through narrow valleys and involved more than 65,000 men, 350 ships and about 700 aircraft from 12 NATO nations. The exercise involved two teams, the 'Blue' team, or intervening forces, and the 'Orange' team forces representing the invading forces, to put the exercise in a realistic perspective, the 'Orange' forces represented the Soviet Army, Navy and Air Force. Although hailed as a resounding success for the 'Blue' forces (NATO alliances), it still left the unanswered question whether in the event of a conflict with Russia, could NATO reinforce northern Norway enough and in sufficient strength to prevent its seizure and occupation by the Russians. The sights and sounds of this exercise remain clear in my mind's eye even today. On completing the exercise, we steamed slowly back to Portsmouth in readiness for the Albion's final deployment to Canada. Unbeknown to the ship's company, HMS Albion was to end her days at sea.

The Albion sailed out of Portsmouth on 10 October 1972, embarking 42 Commando Royal Marines and the following day, we embarked 845 Naval Air Squadron. Sailing north and west and travelling 2374 nautical miles, we crossed the North Atlantic arriving in Saint John, New Brunswick eight days later. Saint John is a seaport city of the Atlantic Ocean located on the Bay of Fundy in the province of New Brunswick, Canada. On our arrival, we landed 42 Commando for exercises ashore with Canadian forces. We remained at sea and two days later, we docked in Halifax, Nova Scotia, for a nine-day visit hosted by HMCS *Stadacona*. Nova Scotia lies in eastern Canada and is the most populous of Canada's four Atlantic Provinces. It is the country's second most densely populated province and second smallest province by area. The peninsula that makes up Nova Scotia's mainland is connected to the rest of North America by the Isthmus of Chignecto, on which the province's land border with New Brunswick is located. The province borders the Bay of Fundy to the west and the Atlantic Ocean to the south and east, and is separated from Prince Edward Island and the island of New Foundland by the Northumberland and Cabot straits, respectively. While in Nova Scotia, we travelled to Halifax and checked out the vibrant Halifax Waterfront. This bustling harbour has a plethora of bars, restaurants, shops, entertainment, and museums and was a frequent port of call during our stay. Nova Scotia is very picturesque and boasts stunning national parks too. Unfortunately, it was during our time in Nova Scotia that the realisation kicked in that when we returned to Portsmouth, not only was HMS

Albion completing her service for the Royal Navy, but all of the crew would be leaving for different ventures. It was during our time in Nova Scotia that my re-deployment papers were issued and I found that I was to be posted to HMS Drake Plymouth. I recall the very sad feeling that we, the crew had at this time. Our lives had been intrinsically linked to the ship for over two years and the parting would be heart retching.

On 31 October, HMS Albion began her slow passage along the Saint Lawrence Seaway. The Saint Lawrence Seaway is a system of locks, canals, and channels in Canada and the United States that permits oceangoing vessels to travel from the Atlantic Ocean to the Great Lakes of North America, as far inland as Duluth, Minnesota, at the western end of Lake Superior. We arrived in Montreal two days later. At Montreal, we embarked 150 sea cadets. The following morning, we sailed from Montreal to Quebec. The sea cadets were set ashore and later that evening set sail again. We called in to Saint John where we recovered 42 Commando and finally departed Canadian waters on 15 November, heading East across the North Atlantic. At 0800 on 22 November, HMS Albion anchored in Plymouth Sound and disembarked 42 Commando, 845 Naval Air Squadron and Kangaw Flight RM.

Sailing from Plymouth the next day, HMS Albion entered Portsmouth Harbour at 1430 on 24 November 1972, flying her paying-off pennant, with a fly-past by 845 Naval Air Squadron. On entering Portsmouth Dockyard, the last procedure Alpha was carried out. Thousands of people had lined the coastline to salute HMS Albion and her crew. Flags were waving, bands were playing, guns were fired and loud cheers could be heard for miles. I remember just how emotional the whole event was, tears filled my eyes and my body shook with pride. On docking, the usual activities then began before disposal of the ship: We spent several weeks de-ammunitioning, returning equipment, and holding the last ship's company dance (ashore). The wardroom held their paying-off ball and, day by day there was an exodus of members of the ship's company going to their new deployments, leaving a skeleton crew on board to complete final tasks.

I recall packing all of my gear and having most of it sent directly to HMS Drake. I prepared to leave the ship carrying as little as possible. Seeing our mess emptied gave a real sinking feeling to the stomach, after all this had been my home for such a long time and so far, I had had my greatest adventures from this very place. Memories came flooding back of joining to the ship in Malta and of

164

the places I had subsequently visited. I was not alone in being tearful at leaving this place and if it had been at all possible, would have stayed here for the rest of my days. Before leaving the ship, I visited my old work places, the forecastle, ship's radio room and other insignificant compartments of the ship. Leaving Portsmouth dockyard was also traumatic. I remember walking, no marching past HMS Victory, stopping to salute before heading for the main gate. I turned one last time to see HMS Albion sitting magnificent in her moorings and gave her one last salute. My last salute was to the dockyard as I passed through her magnificent stone and metal fortress buildings before walking towards the railway station. I was now no longer part of HMS Albion but I was part of her history and I was still part of her last crew. From the dockyard, I proceeded to make my way where I would board a train for home and leave before starting the next phase of my career in the Royal Navy at HMS Drake Plymouth. Leaving HMS Albion impacted on me so much that it affected my career choices from then on.

Chapter Nineteen
Shore Base

Going home on leave should always be a joyful experience. Seeing family, old friends and loved ones is always good. Keeping in touch with the past helps to remind you of the journey's you have taken, whether good or bad and going home always provides a time to reflect. Sadly, as I travelled home, I was not feeling joyful. In fact, I was rather depressed. I had this overwhelming sense of loss. I had lost my beloved ship; my mess, which had been my comfort zone and had lost the vast majority of my shipmates and friends. Living in close proximity with people on a day to day basis, 24 hours per day and over a prolonged period of time cements strong bonds. We had been trained to rely on each other, to support each other and be prepared to die for each other if necessary. The breaking of this attachment came as a shock; no one had prepared me for just how painful this break-up would be. It is strange that when at home; I also felt the loss of past friends when at school and college. When moving away from an area, you lose contact with old past friends and even when you meet up, life takes you in different directions and thus you feel a further sense of loss. I couldn't wait for my leave to end and to return to my new normality, being with like-minded people and serving in the navy.

Returning to Devonport would not be the same as returning to my old ship. The Naval base at Devonport is nicknamed 'Guz' and always referred to as Guz by serving matelot's. It is believed that the nickname originated from the Hindu word for 'Yard' (as in measurement), as sailors have always referred to the Dockyard as just the 'yard'.

HM Naval Base Devonport is the home port of the Devonport Flotilla and is one of three operating bases in the United Kingdom. Devonport is the largest naval base in Western Europe. At one time, the dockyard built ships for the navy but shipbuilding ceased at Devonport in the early 1970s, although ship maintenance work has continued. From 1934, the naval barracks on the site was named HMS Drake. Travelling from home to Plymouth I sat on the train thinking about my time at sea, wondering when I would be allowed to re-join a sailing vessel and what type of vessel it would be. Maybe I would be posted back to carriers, or to destroyers or even frigates. I sincerely hoped that it would be a ship that travelled far and one which was not too small. I hoped and prayed that I would not be posted to minesweepers or the like, they being far too small for me.

On arriving at Drake, I checked in at the gatehouse and was given directions to where I would be housed. HMS Drake is huge. The ship, (all shore bases belonging to the navy are classed as ships) housed its own church, police station and armoury. My time at HMS Drake was taken up mainly with duties on the main gate, checking the identities of the numerous people travelling in and out of the base. Thousands of people worked in HMS Drake and in Devonport Docks; not only naval personnel, but many civilians too. The work on the main gate was tedious and monotonous but still good because of the company I kept there. My nights off were predominantly taken up by going into Plymouth and particularly Union Street. Union Street in Plymouth is a long straight street connecting the city centre to Devonport, the naval base and docks. Originally the home of wealthy people, it later became an infamous red-light district and the location of most of the city's night-life. During the mid-1970s, Union Street was the place to be with so many pubs, clubs and scrumpy houses (pubs that only sold Cider). Strangely, I was drawn more to the old scrumpy houses than I was to the night clubs. The only problem with going to scrumpy houses is that it is not necessarily good for your health. Many a time I could not recall getting back to the barracks and many a morning I woke up feeling very much the worse for wear. My saving grace came in two different ways, firstly in that I had requested to be trained as a ship's diver and secondly, a cousin and her husband had moved to Plymouth from the Midlands because of career advancement for my cousin's husband.

In relation to my cousin's move to Plymouth, they moved to the lovely quiet suburb of Modbury, which is about 12 miles outside Plymouth. On numerous occasions, my cousin's husband would pick me up after work and take me to their home. The location within village of Modbury where they lived was very quiet and peaceful. I would stay with them overnight or for a few days. It was like being home away from home and of course, we had much in common in terms of family and past history. Occasionally, I was called upon to babysit, which I didn't mind in the least. Feet up, watching TV and having drinks available was all that I wanted at this time. Eileen and Alan were great hosts. I am not sure just how much they enjoyed me visiting them, but I certainly enjoyed staying at their home.

When I was called to take the ship's diving course, things had to change. I was not able to visit my cousin quite so often and I had to concentrate very much on the course. Officers and Ratings from all branches of the navy could apply to become a ships diver but each applicant had to first take a one-day aptitude test. The test concentrated on the applicant's swimming ability and their suitability for diving. On the morning of the test, our group were first taken for a thorough medical, followed by a fitness test which involved circuit training and endurance training. We were then taken to the swimming pool where we had to swim fifty lengths of the pool within a given time frame. We were expected to retrieve objects from the bottom of the pool and show that we could hold our breath underwater for the duration of two minutes. I was surprised to find some of the applicants being rejected at this stage. We then had to take a maths test to establish that we would be able to calculate times and pressures. During this first evening, we were then gathered together and informed who would be put forward for the course. I was elated when I was told that I had achieved the highest score of the day. I knew that the swimming and holding my breath had not been a problem and I had been able to find and retrieve objects in the fastest time. It had also been recognised that I had been able to remain submerged longer than all of the other candidates when searching for the smallest of items. I was told that I came within the top three for physical fitness and in the maths test. This gave me such a boost of confidence as I had beaten officers and other ratings that, on observation, looked far fitter than me. There were only six candidates chosen to start the four-week course, which consisted of basic compressed air (open-circuit) diving, extensive instruction (and practice) on searching ships bottoms for explosives, as well as instruction in working on ship's hulls, decompression chambers and maintenance of diving equipment. Our first day on this course comprised of gaining knowledge of equipment, getting into the equipment and filling our own breathing apparatus. I say getting into the equipment because we were issued with 'dry' suits rather than 'wet' suits. Dry suits came as an all-in-one suit that had to be accessed through the neck and made of rubber. The only other openings were at the cuffs. Wet suits on the other hand were made of a sponge-like fabric and were frequently made in two pieces. Wet suits trap water inside the material which is then warmed through body heat. This then keeps the diver warm. Dry suits prevented water from entering because of their tight fit and only the air inside keeps the diver warm. Dry suits are definitely not as warm as wet suits and do tend to limit manoeuvrability.

We spent several days doing open circuit diving in the confines of the swimming pool and practicing exploration and maintenance on mock-ups of parts of ships. We also had to experience decompression by staying within the decompression chamber for a considerably long time. The decompression chamber held six people at any one time. A diving chamber is a container for human occupation, which has an entrance that is sealed to hold an internal pressure significantly higher than ambient pressure; a pressurised gas system controls the internal pressure, and a supply of breathing gas provided for the occupants. There are two main functions for diving chambers. Firstly, as a simple form of submersible that transports divers underwater and provides a temporary base and retrieval system in deep waters. The second as a land, ship or offshore platform-based hyperbaric chamber system, this artificially reproduces the hyperbaric conditions under the sea. Internal pressures above normal atmospheric pressure, is provided for diving-related applications such as saturation diving and diver decompression. We then had to transfer our learned knowledge gained in the indoor pool to open waters.

Our first day in open water was not diving. We had to jump into the sea from a jetty, then swim across the mouth of a river to the opposite side, grab a handful of grass from the embankment and return to our starting positions at the jetty. The water was freezing and the shock of just jumping in took your breath away. The distance from one side of the river to the other was about a mile or so and the wind factor also played its part. Small waves and a strong current moved you further away from the target area and so, the swim took far longer than anticipated. At the far end and before the embankment were areas of thick, slimy, black silt. Any weight on the silt saw you beginning to sink. This caused panic in some and a rescue boat was on hand to retrieve the strugglers. Lying flat, we had to worm our way across the embankment in order to grab hold of any grass that we could fine. Our hands were so cold that we had to re-heat them using our mouths. We were too cold to blow warm air on our hands, so had to place our fingers in our mouths to regain functioning. This then enabled us to grab the required grass from the embankment. The grass was not truly grass, but small reeds that resembled grass and which was green. When we eventually got hold of the grass, the only way that we could ensure we made it back to the other side with our treasure, was to put it in our mouths or to stick the grass in the neck part of our dry suit. For those who didn't put the grass in their mouths or in their wet suits and who preferred to carry the grass in their hands had a tendency to lose their quarry on the return crossing. When those who had chosen to carry their grass in their hands got back to the starting point, they found that their grass had floated away down the river and out to sea. Those who didn't return with their grass were immediately told to re-swim the estuary and complete the task as was their instruction. By the end of the first morning of our outdoor activity, we were freezing cold and exhausted. During the afternoon, metal items were dropped off the jetty and we were given goggles to help retrieve these. We were informed that the average depth was between 20 and 30 foot deep. This meant holding your breath for considerably longer than the two minutes we had practiced in the pool. Retrieving items from the depths in sea water is very much harder than in a swimming pool as the visibility was down to zero. Searching along the bottom is also quite scary. Your mind plays tricks and you begin to believe that there are nasty creatures hiding in the mud getting ready to pounce and to bite your fingers.

When we finally returned to our sleeping quarters, we all spent a very long time just standing in the showers before trying to get out of our dry suits. After re-gaining body warmth, we had to help each other get out of the rubber suits and wash them completely to make sure that no dirt was visible. The dry suits had to be dried inside out to make sure that the inside was properly dry for the next day, and then sprinkled liberally with talc before turning them the right way out. That night, I believe everyone was in bed and fast asleep by 8:30 pm and many were not looking forward to the next day.

The next few days saw us all donning our breathing apparatus and entering the water until the air ran out. We had to learn how to equalise our tanks and had to remain submerged going down to lower levels after re-filling our tanks. During the third week, we spent much of our time sitting on the bottom of the river next to a chain that was anchored by a block of cement. We had to descend taking with us a hammer, chisel and a piece of ¼" chain. At the bottom, we were expected to chisel through one link of chain before our task was complete. In the cold and dark, we chiselled and chiselled, resurfacing, topping up with air then descending again to continue chiselling the chain. I cannot recall if anyone actually completed the task and actually cut through the chain, but measurements were taken of the depth to which the chain had been part severed.

Our final week was spent within the dockyard actually working on the bottom of ships. In some cases, we had to remove barnacles and other crustaceans, carry out repairs, including welding underwater, and removing dummy mines which had been placed by our instructors. We were also taken out to the 'Break Water'. The Break Water is an artificial reef placed out in the sound to help reduce waves coming into the dockyard during inclement weather. Diving down to the break water, we found hundreds of very large concrete blocks which had been placed there over the years and some of the original rocks which had been placed at the time of the break water's construction. It was notable just how many rocks and concrete blocks had moved by the power of the sea, lifting the blocks as if they were feathers blowing in the wind.

On completion of our four-week course, we had a passing out parade. Only four of the original group had made it. On returning to our ship or shore establishment, we were now fully qualified 'Ships Divers'. In order to maintain our new status, we were required to dive for at least 120 minutes during each four-month period and to prove that were still able to carry out work as instructed. Our incentive was that we were given divers' pay, an extra bonus to our basic pay.

Returning back to duty was not only a relief (not getting cold and wet every day), but was also quite a proud moment, as I had achieved something that many others could not or would not ever achieve. My work at the main gate continued until six months later, I was called to the Joss's office and informed that I was being transferred. I had hoped that this transfer was to another sea going post as I had been putting in numerous requests to return to sea, but my hopes were dashed. I was very clearly informed that I would have to remain on terra firma for at least another two years before I would be allowed back to sea going duties and that even after this time, I could be made to stay on a land based ship for even longer. My heart sank at this news and I fell into quite a depressed state of mind. I was told that within the next month or so, I would be deployed to HMS Dryad.

Chapter Twenty
HMS Dryad

After being at HMS Drake for almost a year, and having been in the Navy for over three years, I was transferred to HMS Dryad. HMS Dryad was a Royal Naval complex which provided combined tactical training (CTT). Dryad was a multi-platform force level trainer and was located in Southwich Park. The CTT was the UK's only shore-based environment available to the Royal Navy in which multi-threat; multi-platform training exercises could be conducted. The purpose of this base was to provide training to staff in operational weapon systems on board RN warships. Simulators recreated operational rooms which were located in many of the naval vessels. Any conceivable war-like threat scenario could be simulated and actual world events re-created. Each warship's operations room was authentically replicated together with all ships' sensors, weapons and voice and data communications. This made HMS Dryad a highly classified base.

Several ships' crews could train at the same time, either operating separately or in companion with each other. It was probably the largest Maritime Warfare Simulator in Europe. The CTT facility was at the time of my arrival just being completed, becoming fully operational in 1974. All Royal Naval crews of major warships would pass through the CTT at some point during their careers, sometimes returning many times for further retraining or when they changed ship type. Specific training exercises would take place before all major deployments were carried out. Joint training was also carried out at this facility involving NATO allies and especially the US navy.

Dryad was different to other naval bases. Located in Southwick village, Hampshire, it lies about one-mile north of Portsmouth's northern border. All of the homes and farms within the village form part of an estate, all apart from the Church Lodge. Southwick was initially the site of Southwick Priory, built in the twelfth century. On the Dissolution of Monasteries during the Reformation, the estate, including the village, was granted to John White, servant to Sir Thomas Wriothesley.

The parish of Southwick is very much considered a typical English village, surrounded by woodlands and undulating country. It was said that the parish contained over 725 acres of woodland and was part of the forest of Bere, which lies to the north. Southwick Park also covers a wide area and HMS Dryad forms most of the park. The river Wallington runs through the parish as well as some of the rivers tributaries. The village lies almost in the centre of the parish, to the east of the junction of the Wallington with one of its tributaries, the main village street running parallel with the south-western boundary of the park.

Southwick House is a relatively new manor house completed in 1813. This house was gutted by fire in 1838, and was renovated and rebuilt by 1841. The house and part of the estate was requisitioned by the government during WWII, when the house was Eisenhower's SHAEF headquarters for operation Overlord, the cross-channel invasion of Normandy. The house has been used by various branches of the armed forces, including HMS Dryad, ever since.

Southwick is rare in that the village is still entirely owned by the Southwick Estate (except for Church Lodge). The most obvious sign of this is that all the houses, except manor houses, have dark, red-painted front doors – a condition laid down in the tenancy agreements. The only exceptions to this are the White House, the residence of the vicar and Church Lodge. The only shop within the village was Southwick Village Stores and there were two pubs. The Golden Lion, which was the unofficial officers, mess during WWII. The lounge bar of the Golden Lion (it is said), was also used by Eisenhower, Bradley, and numerous other American generals during WWII and was also frequented by Montgomery, Prince Philip and Earl Mountbatten. The other pub in the village was the Red Lion, mostly used by us ratings but only infrequently.

Buses to and from the village were infrequent too, having only two bus services per day. It is about 13 miles from Southwick to Portsmouth and the journey took about an hour each way. Taxi services were available from Portsmouth, but to get a taxi from Southwick was nigh on impossible. Isolated, remote and what seemed as far from the sea as possible, I was joining HMS Dryad for the foreseeable future.

Arriving back in Portsmouth, I was picked up in a Royal Naval Mini Bus and was driven to Dryad. Although not that far from Portsmouth, the journey seemed endless. On entering the grounds, we drove for what seemed to be a mile along a long drive to the main gate, then onward to the main administration building. After the formalities of officially joining the shore base, I was given directions to what was to be my home for the next two years. The accommodation block was at the very far end of the base and although very new, was quite clinical. My mess, which could accommodate six people, only housed two people, myself and a killick. Unpacking and making my bed was quite a lonely experience. The other guy was working and I was not going to meet him for several hours. I looked out of the window of my mess and all I could see was trees. The view was nice, but not what I had expected. Feeling degenerated; I made my way back to the administration block where I was given instruction about rules, regulation and where my post was to be. I was presented with a map of base and told to equate myself with the base and then to report to the chief at my work station. I was to spend the next year as part of the maintenance department. Although Southwick village was beautiful and picturesque and HMS Dryad very clean, modern and well run, I knew instantly that I would never be able to settle here. My heart sank.

After walking around the base for an hour or so, I had found the most important places; the NAAFI shop and the bar. I also located an old navy double decker bus that had been converted to a cafe and run by an ex-matelot and his wife. I didn't realise at the time, that this double decker was to be a place I would visit daily and where I would get a sausage and runny egg sandwich and coffee, each and every day. Retuning to my mess, I lay on the bed until my roommate arrived. Conversation with him was at a minimal and I soon realised that I would be spending many hours alone in the mess as he was married and every Friday evening, he would go home to his wife, not returning until Monday morning. The only time he was really in the mess was at night for sleeping and at weekends when his duties called for him to be there. This was not a happy start for me.

The next day, I reported to my work station where I was introduced to the guys I would be working with. The work was tedious and quite boring; mainly cleaning around the base and occasionally fixing stuff that had broken down. When work was slacking, we had the wonderful task of painting the coal white. Why we did this I still have no idea, but I expect that it was because aesthetically, the coal looked pleasing being white rather than black. Coal was used in the boiler house providing heating for the base. On occasions, I did have the pleasure of being the 'stocker' in the boiler house for the day.

Dryad was also the training base for 'Radar Operators' (RP's), therefore we had quite a few nearly new recruits on the base. Being part of the ship's company meant that we very rarely mixed with those doing their specialist training.

During the evenings, most of our time was spent in the NAAFI bar, as the pubs in the village were mainly used by the officers and their families. Here in the NAAFI, I met two of my closest friends, Schrader and Brownie. Both were named Paul, so it was either calling them by their surnames or by Paul S and Paul B. Initially, I bonded with Brownie, who was a Killick RP and who was in charge of one of the messes where the new recruits were housed. Brownies mess room had been converted (by him) into a 'home from home'. He had decorated his mess room and placed soft furnishing all around, as well as a TV, fridge and three-piece suit. Brownie was from Bournemouth and like me had lost his father at a very early age. We spent some happy times together in his quarters where we would cook up food and enjoy watching television. Occasionally we would have runs ashore to Portsmouth or into nearby Havant. A few times, we went to Bournemouth to visit his mother, who lived alone in a very small flat. I felt sad each time we visited his mother because of the poverty she seemed to live in. However, Brownie's mother was always welcoming and always pleased to see us both. Bournemouth is blessed with having seven glorious miles of idyllic coastline. Bournemouth is famed as having one of the finest beaches in England, with wide and soft golden sands. Although the English Channel isn't known for its warmth, Bournemouth does have a microclimate creating some of the warmest waters around the UK. There was certainly lots do in Bournemouth, like surfing, kayaking and using paddle boards. However, our time on the beach was focused on sunbathing when the weather was kind enough and swimming, which we both loved.

Back on base, I continued to feel that I needed to get away from shore base and return to sea. I continually put in requests to return to active service but was continually denied. The only real saving grace was that the base had its own stables. Horse riding is a far cry from any other activities provided by the navy, but here was the exception. I spent many happy hours volunteering in the stables, cleaning tack, mucking out, feeding and learning to ride and jump. One of my favourite times was when I was allowed to take one of the horses and to ride around their cross country run. This course followed the perimeter of the base and went through wooded areas as well as meadows. Jumps had been strategically placed around the course which allowed my horsemanship to develop considerably. I frequently rode a horse called Sheba, a white calm horse who appeared to have liked me from our first meeting. I would spend lots of time with Sheba, cleaning her stall, taking her special treats, and grooming her for hours on end. Sheba became my counsellor, listening to me whine about just how unhappy I was to be stuck on a shore base.

There were happy times, but these times were few and far between. Boredom was making my life hell. If I remained around the base at weekends, Sheba would also be with me, especially on Sunday mornings, when we would be out hacking. To join the horsey group for hacking, I had to be appropriately attired; therefore, I went out, purchased a hacking jacket, jodhpurs, knee length riding boots and crop and a hard hat. I certainly looked the part, but never felt like one of the group who were mainly made up of officers, their wives and their children. I was the only rating in the group. However, these Sunday rides were fun, if only to spend time with Sheba.

At weekends, when I didn't have the money to go home, or I didn't want to be at the base, I would go to Portsmouth and stay at the Royal Sailors Rest. Spending time in the local pubs and frequently hanging around outside of the dockyard gates. How I longed to be able to go back inside the docks to re-join my ship. I also frequently met up with old naval and civilian friends who in some ways alleviated the tensions I was experiencing but also by adding to the tensions by telling me where they were based and the good times they were having. When I told them about my deployment, you could see their facial expressions change and could understand why I wanted to get away from the place. A couple of my civilian friends would invite me to their place for drinks and the occasional dinner, but even their input was not depleting my feeling of wow. They too seemed to be living far more exciting lives than I was.

My first year in Dryad was nothing more than purgatory. Request after request was submitted to have me redeployed. My requests falling on deaf ears and with each request being told verbally, 'no way'.

Chapter Twenty-One
The Bright Lights and Departure

During the second year at Dryad, I was moved from my work place in the maintenance department to become part of the security squad, protecting the base and ensuring that undesirables did not enter. My main duty was to be sentry on the main gate. Rather than working nine to five, I was put back on watches; Afternoon, First and Mornings and Dogs, Middle Forenoon. No longer would I be wearing number eight's and overalls, but would have to wear full dress uniform, boots, a white belt with a bayonet and white spats. I would also be carrying a loaded sub machine gun; after all, this was a highly sensitive base which was full of secret equipment. My lazy evenings with Brownie were coming to an end as I would not be able to see him quite so much; neither would I be able to visit his mother in Bournemouth. My friendship with Schrader would develop more now as Schrader was also part of the security team.

Not long after being told of my impending move to security, Brownie was also given the news that he was being re-deployed. Brownie had been at Dryad for over three years and he was heading back to sea. How I envied him and immediately put in for a transfer for myself. Once again my application was rejected.

On my first watch on the main gate, Schrader met me at the gatehouse and introduced me to one of my opposite numbers who was covering the other watches. My opposite number passed on the paperwork to Schrader who then signed them off and put my name on the list as duty guard. As soon as my opposite number had gone, Schrader went through what had to be done when I was on watch. Every person who approached the main gate had to have their ID's checked and had to be signed in. High ranking officers, dignitary and personnel from the Department of Defence who had pre-arranged meetings were given on a list with an expected time of arrival (ETA) next to their names, position and who they were meeting with. All officers and dignitary had to be greeted with a salute, ID's checked and their arrival phoned through to the main admin block before the barriers to the base could be opened. Each officer and rating entering the base once checked had to sign in before access was given. Any suspicious characters had to be reported immediately to the admin block and I had to be in a state of preparedness just in case someone attempted to enter the base illegally. Schrader stayed with me throughout the watch and told me that he would be with me for the first week. After that, he would be calling in to check on me from time to time as his role determined.

The first week proved to be a really good week in that Schrader and I formed a sound bond. I found out that Schrader, who was from Wales, had a German father and English mother but had been raised in Wales. Both of his parents were dead and after being raised by his grandmother had joined the navy. Sadly, his grandmother had since passed away and he had no one in this country who he could call family. Even with all of this loss in his life, Schrader was always smiling and happy. He made me laugh a lot, particularly when he was trying to say something which had amused him. This was because he got tongue tied and most of what he said was unintelligible. Because Schrader was on the same duty watches as me, we began meeting up in the NAAFI where we would drink together and played pool and darts. We also spent time ashore together, going into Portsmouth on our days off.

Schrader was a really sociable guy and soon made friends with the friends I had, particularly with John Hart and Peter Jones. Schrader was fascinated by their stories of working in the theatre and their stories about different nights out they had in London. After a few meetings with John and Peter, arrangements were made for Schrader and me to join John and Peter in London for a weekend. John had a flat in Highgate and said that he would be happy for us to stay there. Our first weekend in London was just mind-blowing. During the day, Schrader and I would walk around taking in the sights, as neither of us had spent time in London before. At night, we would either join up with John and Peter in a pub near their respective theatres and then on went on to some night clubs, or just go out alone. Late nights out, was something that neither Schrader nor I had done very much while at Dryad. The weekend had been such a great success that we started to plan for more weekends away from the base.

Schrader and I spent weekends in London, Wales, on the Isle of White and at my home in the Midlands. Schrader became close to my family and my friends.

We spent many nights in night clubs deciding on which ones were best and which ones we wouldn't visit again. We both really enjoyed London's bars and clubs and when I couldn't go up to London, Schrader nearly always made his way there or up to my home. He became very much like another brother, supportive and always happy. The only time we really ever argued was when one night in the NAAFI during a disco night, Schrader brought with him a new single, which he had purchased that day. While he was at the bar, I gave the single to the DJ to play. Schrader was not happy with what I had done and got quite upset with me.

Life was getting much better having Schrader about even though I was still very unhappy with being at Dryad. Then the bombshell was dropped. Schrader announced that he had applied to 'buy himself out' of the navy. All service personnel who had served three years or more could apply to buy themselves out of their service should they not wish to complete the full term that they had signed up for. This was devastating news for me. Schrader had decided that he wanted to work in theatre and film and had been having discussions with John and Peter. Peter had introduced Schrader to a producer who worked at the BBC and who had said that once he had left the navy, he would consider Schrader for a job. However, not long after this, the guy from the BBC contacted Schrader informing him that there was a brilliant opportunity coming up and if he wanted to be considered, he would need to think about coming out of the navy fairly quickly. It didn't take long for Schrader to decide and immediately applied to come out of the service. Within weeks, and after Schrader taking his discharge leave, he was working full-time for the BBC.

On base, I was left without any real friends, although I did have mates, things were just not the same. Being alone much of the time, particularly in my sentry box and in the mess caused me to become quite depressed. I approached the First Lieutenant asking for a transfer but was told that this still wasn't possible. It would be another year before I would be allowed back to sea. Considering this, and weighing up how I was feeling psychologically, I decided to follow Schrader in applying to buy myself out of the navy. It took several weeks before my request was finally accepted. I think that the request was accepted mainly because of the amount of other requests I had made for transfers back to sea. And so, in June 1975, I finally left the service of the Royal Navy. It had been five years and one month since joining the navy and I was now 20 years old.

Leaving the navy was so difficult and it took me several years to readjust to civilian life. I still to this day, regret that I had to leave. Had I been given the opportunity to go back to sea, or that my two closest friends had not gone from Dryad, perhaps I would have remained in the service that I loved. Looking back, I truly believe that the navy provided a sound foundation for the rest of my life. Since leaving, I have achieved much and reached the top of my new profession following discharge from Her Majesties Royal Navy. Recently, I made a return visit to Singapore, visiting Sembawang dockyard, reflecting and reminiscing on my time there. I consider myself blessed to have lived, worked, laughed and cried with those people who served beside me and will forever be eternally grateful to the navy for giving me such a great start in life.